Dollar Store Arbitrage

How to Make $100 a Day Selling Dollar Store Finds

By Abigaile L. Hunt

For Beth, with love, Abby Hunt

Legal Information

Disclaimer of Endorsement: References herein to any specific commercial products, processes, or services by trade name, trademark, manufacturer or otherwise, does not constitute or imply its endorsement, recommendation or favoring by the author. No relationship, sponsorship or endorsement between the author and any company is implied by the reference to corporations, brands, trademarks, or trade names in this publication.

This book contains statements and claims relating to the amount of money one can make using these methods. Please understand that these are estimates and projections. The exact amount you can make will depend on your hard work, your experience, resources, and opportunities.

Although the author and publisher have made every effort to ensure that the information in this book was correct at press time, the author and publisher do not assume and hereby disclaim any liability to any party for any loss, damage, or disruption caused by errors or omissions, whether such errors or omissions result from negligence, accident, or any other cause.

Is This Book For You?

For the beginning seller: If you are a beginning seller on Amazon.com but already understand how to list an item and create and send in a shipment, you will find some great Dollar Store strategies in this book. These strategies will help you purchase inventory with a small amount of capital. They'll also help you branch into new product lines that you may not have considered before.

However, this is not a book for the very new seller. If you have NEVER sold anything on Amazon, I recommend going to the Amazon.com home page. Scroll to the bottom of the page and click the link "Sell on Amazon." Amazon has some wonderful video tutorials to help you get started. You do not need to be a registered seller on Amazon to view these videos. There is also a variety of books currently available on how to begin selling on Amazon. If you have never sold on Amazon.com, you will want to create a Seller Account and get an understanding of how to list items for sale before beginning this book. I recommend a Pro Merchant account with Amazon and an understanding of the

Fulfillment by Amazon (FBA) program for the best chance of success.

For the advanced seller. This book will give you strategies that can increase your profits by an average of $36,000 per year. There are tips here that, while suggested for use in dollar stores, may also be effective in your favorite retail and thrift stores. These strategies will help you find new items to purchase with just a small investment and will also help you branch into new product lines that you may not have considered before.

Introduction

For more than sixteen years I have been selling online and I am still surprised when people are shocked that I can make a living with online sales. I am even more surprised when they think I am some mastermind with my finger on the pulse of what's new, what's hot, and what will sell. I must have a crystal ball hidden in my office which allows me to determine what to buy to make the biggest profit. Certainly my experience helps, but the types of items I previously sold on eBay for large profits barely get a second glance these days. The online marketplace is constantly evolving and ever-changing. Savvy sellers keep their eyes open and adjust to that ever-flowing tide of change.

Instead of a crystal ball, I have many practical tools at my disposal and I use the information from these tools to make an informed decision. Sure, there is some "gut instinct" involved, but the wealth of information created from these tools is extremely useful. I would be lost without my smartphone and apps that help me with my product-buying decisions. For example, "Amazon

Seller" is a free app for your phone that lets you scan the barcode (or type in the title) of an item to see if it is selling on Amazon.com and at what price.

Buy low, sell high. There it is, right there, the key to success. But that is also an oversimplification of what is involved. What should you buy? Where can you find it? How much should you buy? How much should you sell it for? Where should you sell it? How do you market it? What is the demand? What will your margin be? What is your return on investment (ROI)? How long should you hold on to it? What if it doesn't sell? Where do you start? Never fear Dear Reader, start here.

Table of Contents

Dollar Store Arbitrage

As we begin with this idea of *Dollar Store Arbitrage*, it makes sense to clearly define just what that is.

A **dollar store** is exactly as the name implies, a store where each item sells for $1.00 (plus tax where applicable). In economic terms it is considered a price-point retailer: thus, a *Dollar Store* will sell each item in its store for $1.00, a *99¢ Store* will sell items for 99¢ each. In the late 1800s *5 & 10-cent Stores* (or dime stores) were a retail success. By the mid-1900s, when stores were no longer able to sell any items for just five or ten cents, they came to be called *Variety Stores* offering good values at low prices. These variety stores transitioned into the dollar stores we see today.

Arbitrage sounds daunting when you read the definition: Arbitrage is the practice of taking advantage of a price difference between two or more markets, striking a combination of matching deals that capitalize upon the imbalance, with the profit being the difference between the market prices. In simpler terms, buy low (from here) and sell high (over there).

My favorite example of arbitrage (though not *dollar store arbitrage*) is that of a happy little tourist shop in New England. Our New England retailer purchases a large assortment of umbrellas for the upcoming spring season. By the end of May, he realizes it has been a particularly dry spring and the summer will only be worse for umbrella sales. He marks them all down 75% to make room for summer merchandise. A lucky arbitrage seller purchases all of these discounted umbrellas and sells them for a profit online. Buyers in soggier markets (like Seattle, for example) will swoop down on his lovely assortment of umbrellas, purchase them online and his profit is in the bank. Certainly, our New England retailer could have sold his stock of umbrellas online, but his main focus is his brick-and-mortar store, so he is more than happy to sell off his stagnant merchandise and move on.

Dollar Store Arbitrage is the process of buying products from dollar stores and selling them online for a profit. That sounds easy, right? But we still have pesky questions about what to buy, where to sell it, margins, ROI, etc. Let's take a look at the options.

For argument's sake, let's assume you have purchased a plush Mickey Mouse toy from a dollar store. (Figure 1) You paid a dollar.

Figure 1

Since you are a reseller, the owner did not charge sales tax. Mickey is sitting in the bag from the dollar store; what can you do with him? If you already own your own brick-and-mortar store, maybe you could sell him there. Or if you have your own website storefront, you could list him for sale there. Assuming you have neither, eBay and Amazon are the most-likely choices for Mickey.

Both are well known, respected ecommerce sites that do not require you to "re-invent the wheel" by creating your own website, marketing your products and attracting millions of potential buyers.

On both eBay and Amazon, you are considered a third-party seller. You are not employed by either of these companies, and at no time do they own your merchandise. I personally sold on eBay for more than 12 years and I was very successful for most of that time. However, the marketplace has changed and Amazon is now a much better fit for me. Amazon has created one of the most advanced fulfillment networks in the world. This gives me the ability to scale my business (grow my business in leaps and bounds) with Amazon's FBA program. With Fulfillment by Amazon (FBA) you store your products in Amazon's fulfillment centers, and they pick, pack, ship, and provide customer service for these products.

It is not necessary for you to use Amazon's FBA program. You can store your own merchandise and still sell on Amazon as a third-party seller. This is a more cost-effective option because you do not pay Amazon for storage or Pick and Pack fees, but I feel that the benefits of selling with FBA are worth every penny. FBA handles customer service and returns for Amazon.com orders. Listings are displayed with the *Amazon Prime* logo, so customers know that packing, delivery, customer service and returns are all handled by Amazon. Amazon is known for its excellent customer service and they want buyers to shop with confidence any time they make a purchase from Amazon.com. The condition of the item and its timely delivery are guaranteed under the Amazon A-to-Z Guarantee. They even extend this guarantee to purchases from third-party sellers when payment is made via the Amazon.com website. This is a HUGE advantage! This is why I recommend selling through Amazon's FBA program 99% of the time. This book will focus on FBA selling and the examples I use will assume the fees associated with FBA. Just keep in mind that it is just one option available to you.

Let's get back to our Mickey Mouse toy.

In my opinion, Mickey is worth at least a few dollars for our time so we want to try to sell him on Amazon for at least $10. After deducting Amazon fees, our payout from Amazon will be $5.83. After we subtract our original $1 cost, we will see a profit of approximately $4.83 for Mickey. If you assume that overhead costs, boxes, tape, labels and other business expenses are no more than $ .83 (certainly not that high per piece but stay with me here), you are looking at a profit of $4 on your initial $1 investment! There is no interest rate that I know of that will give you that kind of return on your investment.

Now let's see if Mickey is currently listed in Amazon's catalog. Our first step when considering any item to buy for resale on Amazon is to check to see if the item is already listed on Amazon (already in their catalog). The long way to do this is to go to www.amazon.com and key in the UPC code from Mickey's tag.

Figure 2

When entering the UPC code, be sure to include the small digits at the beginning and end (Figure 2). I have used a generic UPC in this example but if we enter the UPC code from our toy, there are three possible outcomes.

First, he may be listed already. In that case, the product page will appear (Figure 3):

Figure 3

By entering the UPC code, you find that the exact toy is already listed on Amazon. This is the easiest result and you can make your buying decision from here. He is already being sold at around your price point, currently $9.47. So this looks like a profitable item to list. We can also find other valuable information on this page, like the fact that there are currently only 22 other sellers offering this toy as "new." When you consider how popular Mickey Mouse is, you can feel confident that 22 other sellers is not a big concern, especially since further research reveals that 15 of those sellers are selling at a higher price than you are. If there were only 22 other stores in the entire US that sold the same toy that you did, you wouldn't consider that much competition would you?

Next, let's suppose we scanned the UPC and got no results (Figure 4):

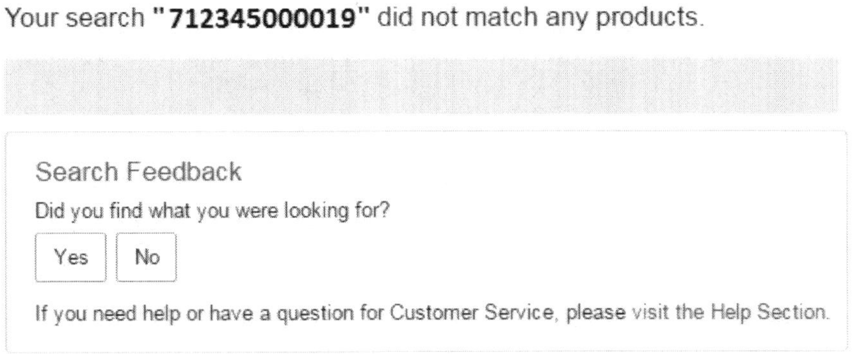

Your search **"712345000019"** did not match any products.

Search Feedback
Did you find what you were looking for?

| Yes | No |

If you need help or have a question for Customer Service, please visit the Help Section.

Figure 4

This result does not necessarily mean that your toy is not listed on Amazon, but it does mean that you need to do more research. Now you need to search for Mickey through a keyword search. This is VERY IMPORTANT because lazy scanners will pass up a profitable product because they entered the UPC and didn't get a result. For Mickey, there are hundreds of possible keyword combinations you can use. On the other hand, if you had an electronic item in your hand, it would be very specific and easier to search by keywords.

For your Mickey Mouse toy, you would start with the basic keywords first: the product name, size and other identifying information. In this case, **Disney Mickey**

Mouse 9 inch Plush. You should always use numbers but spell out measurements rather than using symbols such as quotation marks (") for inches. This is how Amazon formats the information in their titles.   As you can see, our keyword search returned 221 results. Clearly, Mickey Mouse is a popular guy, but you probably already knew that.

Of the six listings shown in Figure 5, can you find the listing that matches your Mickey Mouse toy exactly?

Disney 9" Mickey Mouse Plush
by Disney

$8.99
Only 1 left in stock - order soon.

More Buying Choices
$4.47 new (21 offers)

★★★★☆ ▾ 5

FREE Shipping

Product Features
Soft & adorable 9" tall Mickey Mouse plush

Toys & Games: See all 176 items

Disney Parks Baby Mickey And Minnie - 9 Inch Long Pile Plush With Rattle Inside - Disney Parks Exclusive & Limited...
by Disney

$60.86 + $7.99 shipping
Only 3 left in stock - order soon.

More Buying Choices
$60.86 new (2 offers)

Product Features
... Disney Parks Baby Mickey And Minnie Long Pile Plush ..

Toys & Games: See all 176 items

Disney Mickey Mouse Mini Bean Bag Plush
by Disney

$9.45 $34.95 ✓Prime
Only 15 left in stock - order soon.

More Buying Choices
$2.27 new (22 offers)

★★★★☆ ▾ 39

Manufacturer recommended age: 5 - 70 Years

Product Features
Measures 9" high. Officially licensed Disney product.

Toys & Games: See all 176 items

Disney Mickey Mouse Clubhouse Plush Beanz Mickey
by Dream International

$17.78 + $4.72 shipping
Only 1 left in stock - order soon.

More Buying Choices
$17.78 new (2 offers)

Product Features
Approx 9 inch

Toys & Games: See all 176 items

Disney Mickey Mouse Mini Bean Bag Plush - Holiday - 9"
by Disney

$21.95 ✓Prime
Only 1 left in stock - order soon.

Product Features
.. 9" H (ear to toe) Embroidered ... Magic Holiday Plush Collection ..

Toys & Games: See all 176 items

Mini Bean Bag Mickey Mouse Plush Toy -- 9" H
by Disney

$10.75 ✓Prime
Only 4 left in stock - order soon.

More Buying Choices
$3.40 new (19 offers)

★★★★☆ ▾ 11

Product Features
A great match for our Minnie Mouse Mini Bean Bag Plush

Toys & Games: See all 176 items

Figure 5

The third listing down looks very much like your toy and by clicking on that listing, you get all of the information needed to determine that it is EXACTLY the plush toy that you want to sell. "Close" is NOT good enough here. Your toy must be exactly the same as the Amazon product page, so be sure to check the existing listing completely. You are looking for an exact match here so be sure to check all related photos, bullet points and descriptions from the Amazon product page with your product.

Your third possible result when you enter the UPC for this toy is that it simply does not exist in Amazon's extensive product list. In this case, you will have to create your own listing for this toy. There are many schools of thought on when it is profitable to create your own listing. In general, I agree with the opinion that you should create a product listing when you know you can make at least $100 selling quantities of the product. If you can get your hands on 25 of these Mickey Mouse toys, your profit would be $4 each, so creating your own listing makes sense. I will discuss HOW to create your own listings in a later chapter.

As I said earlier when you entered the UPC on Amazon at home, this was the long way to research your item. Preferably, while you are in the store, you want to make decisions using a barcode scanning app to avoid making unprofitable purchases. Most smartphones can scan a barcode quickly and immediately return the information you need to make a buying decision. If a scanning app is not currently on your phone, it takes just a minute to go to your app store and download one. "Barcode Scanner" is fast, easy and reliable. It can scan UPCs, ISBN codes on books and QR codes (Quick Response Codes that look like a grid and store lots of data).

Any barcode scanner will work together with a free app called "Amazon Seller," which gives you important information that you can use to make your buying decision. Personally I prefer a subscription-based app from ScanPower which provides the information in a layout that I find easier to read and evaluate.

Here is an example of results obtained using the Amazon Seller app (Figure 6).

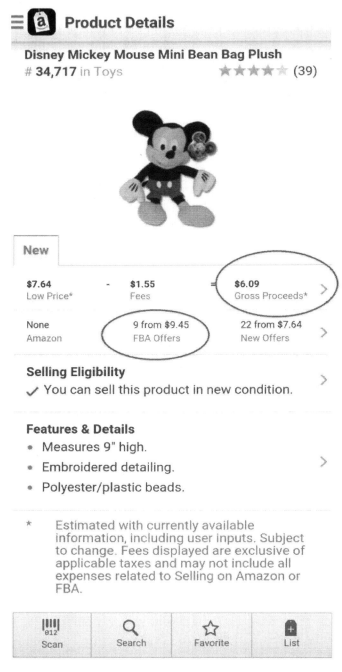

Figure 6

If you look at Figure 6, you will see that I have circled "$6.09 Gross Proceeds." I find this to be a little misleading because you will not be pocketing $6.09. That amount is based on the seller (you) shipping the product directly to the customer if you sell this item for $7.64 on Amazon. The second circle in Figure 6 reads, "9 from $9.45 FBA Offers." This means that the FBA sellers are selling this item for $9.45 so this is a better number for comparison. It does not, however, tell you what your net proceeds will be.

If you click the small arrow to the right of "Gross Proceeds" you will bring up a second page of Product Details in the Amazon Seller App (Figure 7).

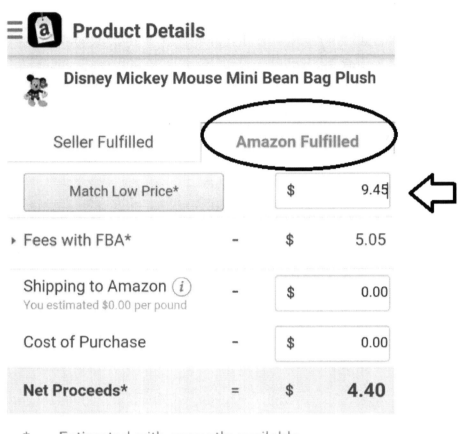

Product Details

Disney Mickey Mouse Mini Bean Bag Plush

Seller Fulfilled	Amazon Fulfilled

Match Low Price*	$	9.45

▸ Fees with FBA* — $ 5.05

Shipping to Amazon (i)
You estimated $0.00 per pound — $ 0.00

Cost of Purchase — $ 0.00

Net Proceeds* = $ **4.40**

* Estimated with currently available information, including user inputs. Subject to change. Fees displayed are exclusive of applicable taxes and may not include all expenses related to Selling on Amazon or FBA.

Figure 7

On this page, you can select the "Amazon Fulfilled" tab and enter $9.45 as the selling price. In this example, the Net Proceeds have been calculated as $4.40. This is still just an estimate, as explained by the note on the bottom of the page, "Estimated with currently available information, including user inputs. Subject to change. Fees displayed are exclusive of applicable taxes and may not include all expenses related to Selling on Amazon or FBA."

I have compared the Amazon Seller app to the ScanPower app and have found that the ScanPower app accurately reflects the actual payout I receive. There are still advantages to the Amazon Seller App. First of all, it is free and it definitely shows whether or not an item is already listed on Amazon. There is also a HUGE advantage to using the Amazon Seller app. It very clearly states your Selling Eligibility: **You can sell this product in new condition**. This is important because some merchandise categories on Amazon are restricted or need prior approval. A complete list of these restrictions and requirements can be found on Amazon.

The Listings Restrictions can be found here: http://www.amazon.com/gp/help/customer/display.html?nodeId=200832290 and the Categories Requiring

Approval can be found here:
http://www.amazon.com/gp/help/customer/display.ht
ml?nodeId=14113001.

Compare Figure 6 and Figure 7 to a screenshot of the ScanPower app (Figure 8). ScanPower keeps the information short, sweet and to the point:

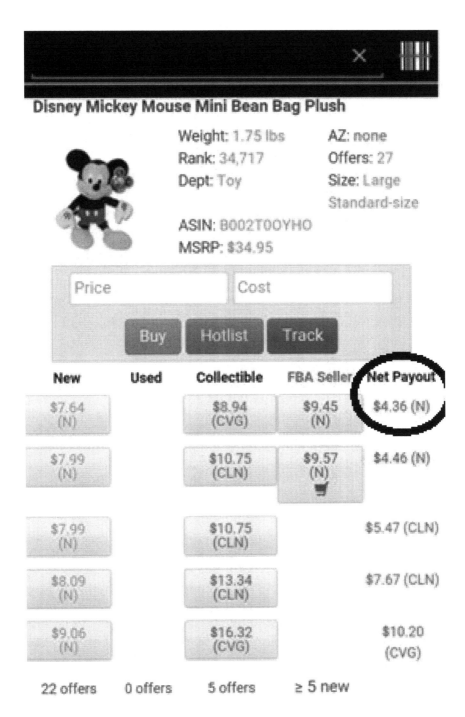

Disney Mickey Mouse Mini Bean Bag Plush

Weight: 1.75 lbs   AZ: none

Rank: 34,717   Offers: 27

Dept: Toy   Size: Large

Standard-size

ASIN: B002TOOYHO

MSRP: $34.95

Price	Cost

Buy   **Hotlist**   **Track**

New	Used	Collectible	FBA Seller	Net Payout
$7.64 (N)		$8.94 (CVG)	$9.45 (N)	$4.36 (N)
$7.99 (N)		$10.75 (CLN)	$9.57 (N)	$4.46 (N)
$7.99 (N)		$10.75 (CLN)		$5.47 (CLN)
$8.09 (N)		$13.34 (CLN)		$7.67 (CLN)
$9.06 (N)		$16.32 (CVG)		$10.20 (CVG)
22 offers	0 offers	5 offers	≥ 5 new	

Figure 8

I have compared this "Net Payout" amount to my statement from Amazon and it is an exact match. This is important to me when I make my buying decisions. ScanPower is a subscription service with a monthly fee, but it has many valuable features. Visit www.scanpower.com to see if it matches your needs. You can get a 5-day trial if you are interested but unsure.

Here are a few of my favorite features when I use the ScanPower app:

(1) I can easily scan a barcode or enter a title or keywords.
(2) Everything displays on one page.
(3) I can see the "Net Payout," which is the exact amount I would put in my pocket after my cost.

Research

When you looked at the listing for the Mickey Mouse toy, there were other pieces of information that you need to look at more carefully when making your buying decision.

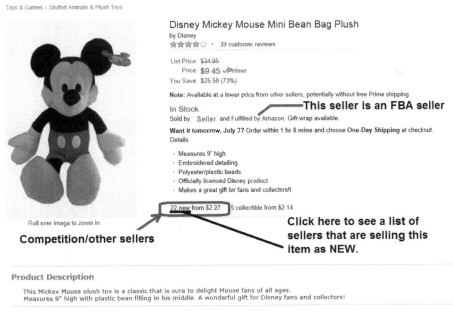

Figure 9

First of all, is Amazon itself a seller of this item? It is difficult to compete with Amazon as a seller. It is not impossible, but the margins here are usually not worth the struggle. I do believe that Amazon does not have an unlimited supply of products and that competing with Amazon can be done, but do so with the right information at hand. Your other competition falls into two distinct groups: other FBA sellers, and third-party sellers. Other FBA sellers represent strong competition but they also help you to determine whether or not an item is worth selling.

When comparing the prices, you want to compare your sales price on Amazon with other FBA sellers. Since your cost for an item is only a dollar, it is possible that you could price your item slightly lower than another FBA seller and still make a healthy profit. In Figure 9, we see that Amazon is NOT a seller of this particular item and that the current price of $9.45 is being offered by another FBA seller. This means that we can price our item at $9.45 and match that lowest sales price and compete directly with another FBA seller.

If you look a little farther down in Figure 9, you will see "22 new from $2.27." This means that there are 22 other sellers, both FBA and other third-party sellers, which are selling this exact item for as low as $2.27 but that number does not include shipping from those other sellers. If you click on the "22 new" you will find that the third-party seller is charging $5.49 for shipping. However, their item does not qualify for Free Two-day shipping or any other Amazon Prime Benefits (because they are not an FBA seller) and it will take an additional four days to receive their item from Illinois. So a buyer could pay $1.69 less for the same item and get it in about a week.

Third-party sellers are basically selling the products on Amazon but they are shipping them from their location, not Amazon's warehouse. The products listed by these sellers do not enjoy the benefits of Amazon Prime. They are less of a competitive factor but still a good way for you to compare prices especially if there are no FBA sellers selling a particular product. Be aware of your competition but don't be discouraged by it. You need some competition to help you determine whether or not a product or product category is profitable. If you find an item at a dollar store that other sellers are only selling for $2, you know that specific item is not profitable, not worth your time, and you can put it down and move on.

Next, in which category is the item listed? Certain products cannot be listed or sold on Amazon.com. Some products may not be listed due to legal or regulatory restrictions (for example, illegal drugs) or per Amazon policy (for example, crime scene photos). For detailed information, see Restricted Products and Listing Restrictions on Amazon's website. For some product categories, sellers are not allowed to create product listings without prior approval from Amazon. Also, sellers may be required to obtain additional approval to list certain products in certain categories.

As of this writing, these categories require prior approval from Amazon:

3D Printed Products
Automotive & Power sports
Beauty
Clothing & Accessories
Collectible Books
Collectible Coins
Entertainment Collectibles
Fine Art
Gift Cards
Grocery & Gourmet Foods
Health & Personal Care
Independent Design
Industrial & Scientific
Jewelry
Luggage & Travel Accessories

Major Appliances
Sexual Wellness
Shoes, Handbags & Sunglasses
Sports Collectibles
Video, DVD, & Blu-ray
Watches
Wine

You can find the requirements needed to get approval on Amazon's Help Pages. They do this to ensure that customers are able to buy with confidence from all sellers on Amazon.com. In addition to these, Amazon has outlined items that are prohibited or restricted for sale on their website. Customers trust that they can always buy with confidence on Amazon.com so products offered for sale on Amazon.com must comply with all laws and regulations as well as with Amazon's policies. The sale of illegal, unsafe, or other restricted products including products available only by prescription is strictly prohibited.

Amazon takes product safety and these restrictions very seriously. Sellers should carefully review the "Examples of Permitted and Prohibited Listings" sections in each Restricted Product category before listing a product. **If you sell a Restricted Product, Amazon may immediately suspend or terminate your selling privileges and destroy inventory in the fulfillment centers without reimbursement.**

In addition, if Amazon determines that a seller's account has been used to engage in illegal activity, remittances and payments may be withheld or forfeited. The sale of illegal or unsafe products can also lead to legal action, including civil and criminal penalties.

Each category that has restrictions is clearly explained on Amazon's Help Pages.

For example, in the **ALCOHOL** category:

Examples of Permitted Listings

    Wine sold by pre-approved sellers

    Food products that contain alcohol for flavor

    Wine and beer making kits and products that do not contain alcohol

    Alcohol-related accessories and products, including corkscrews, decanters and containers

    Alcohol-related memorabilia and collectibles that do not contain alcohol

Examples of Prohibited Listings

    Alcoholic beverages (except from pre-approved wine sellers)

    Liquor licenses

So the bottom line here is to know the specifics of the category that best matches your product. You should know its permissible items and those that are restricted.

This is extremely important and easily found on Amazon's Help Pages.

Once you know whether Amazon is a seller/competitor, what the product category is and if it is restricted, you will look at a product's sales rank. The sales rank of an item on Amazon is not an indication of how popular an item is nor how quickly it will sell but it is an indication of RECENT sales. The top 100 items in a category will have ranks of 1, 2, 3, 4, 5 etc. so a lower number is better. Here is a great example of a top 100 toy. This Pool Float (Figure 10) has a sales rank of 12.

Figure 10

Let's say you found an item like this (Figure 10) that was in the top 100 of its category. This would be a great item to buy, especially at a dollar store! Your cost will only be one dollar for each of that particular item that you can buy. With a sales rank of 12, this item sells roughly 81 times **per day**! As this is a seasonal item, sales may slow down at other times of the year, but this example shows the importance of sales rank in your buying decision, top 100 is awesome, top 1000 is great, a rank of 10,000 is good and the sales decrease from there.

I recently scanned an electronic accessory in my favorite dollar store with a rank of 50! Wow! I bought all eight that were on the rack and asked if they had any more (they didn't). Even if this item slowed down in sales the day after my purchase, it still has an awesome rank and will probably continue to sell well.

I must caution you about Sales Rank, though. Items with a low Sales Rank mean that they have sold recently and is a good indication that the items will sell again. This is why lower Sales Rank items are generally considered a good choice to sell on Amazon. But, keep in mind that just because something has been selling well, doesn't mean it will always sell well. Consider seasonal items that may sell well during certain times of the year but perhaps not at all during other times. See the chapter on movie tie-ins for good examples of this phenomenon.

Key points from this chapter:

1. Look at all available information when making a buying decision.
2. Know the rules of the categories in which you wish to sell.
3. Be aware of any Amazon listing restrictions.

Dollar Store Merchandise

There are more than 50,000 dollar stores in the US. There are corporate owned franchises; *Dollar General, Just A Buck, Dollar Tree* and local "mom 'n pop" single owner stores with names like *Dollar Deals, $1 & Up, Dollar Kraze, Dollar Power*, and *The 99c Store*. They represent a growing trend in cost effective merchandise. Dollar Tree alone had net sales of more than $8 billion in 2014.

Dollar General is not a true dollar store as items can be as high as $19.99, so it is more of a discount store than a true dollar store. For our purposes we will stick to the dollar stores where most of the inventory is $1 or less. Some local stores will price some items $1.49, $1.25 etc. This should not be a major concern but you should be aware of your costs and factor it into your cost of goods.

The inventory at individual dollar stores varies but the major categories are similar in most dollar stores. The top categories of your average dollar store include the following. Impulse items are located near the front of the store including key chains, jewelry, electronic accessories, batteries and snacks.

Party supplies including tableware, decorations, gift wrap and greeting cards can be found down one aisle. Seasonal items take up a large portion of one wall and are stocked and sold in the blink of an eye. With space at such a premium, it is unlikely that you will find seasonal items stocked too far in advance of the holiday. Likewise, the items are sold off quickly after the holiday to make room for the next holiday.

Housewares, tools, school and office supplies, books and gift items flow together along one aisle. Baby products, beauty supplies, hair accessories and toys occupy another aisle. Toys can be found in nearly every aisle and low enough on the shelf so that kids can shop for their own treasures. Finally, personal care, cleaning products and storage containers take up a significant bit of real estate in a dollar store. The variety and quality of products will differ from store to store but nearly every store will have treasures waiting for you to profit from.

Now where do dollar stores get their inventory?

When someone decides to own and operate a dollar store, they have options which make the process a bit easier. There are businesses with the sole purpose of "creating your store." They offer to handle everything beginning with the store layout to cash wrap supplies like cash registers, credit card machines, counters and display units and ending with the inventory the store will carry. There are distributors whose entire clientele is the dollar store industry so they carry a wide range of products in the most popular dollar store categories. They do all of the hard work of purchasing closeout merchandise, purchasing large quantities from wholesalers and navigating purchases from China and other importers.

If you are concerned that you won't find anything to sell from your local dollar store, just take a look at a sample of categories below.

Apparel
Automotive
Baby-Infants
Beauty Accessories
Body Jewelry
Books

Bridal–Wedding

Candles

Cellular Accessories

Costume Jewelry

Crafts

Earrings

Electronics

Fashion Accessories

Figurines

Footwear

Fragrances/Perfumes

Furniture

General Merchandise

Gifts

Groceries/Food Prod.

Hardware

Hats and Caps

Health Products

Holiday/Seasonal

Home Decor

Housewares

Incense

Jewelry

Lawn and Garden

Licensed Merchandise

Lighters

Linens

Lingerie

Novelties

Office Supplies

Pet Accessories

Reading Glasses

Restaurant Supplies

School Supplies

Scrapbook Supplies

Silk Plants

Sporting Goods

Stationery

Sunglasses

T-Shirts

Tools

Toys

Travel

Videos

Wallets

Even though you may not be able to sell in every single one of these categories, there is more than enough variety for you to choose from.

Franchisees and the managers of corporate-owned own stores like Dollar Tree have less direct interaction with their suppliers but the local mom-and-pop-type stores have more control over the items they bring into their stores. One shop owner here in New Jersey carries a unique assortment of products imported from Jordan and Syria that he displays them near his cash registers. They are eye-catching and not something you would normally see in any store, especially a dollar store so they sell well for him. He has already made the international connection for the importing of these products which keeps his costs low so that he can sell them for a dollar. He fills the rest of his store with products from the dollar store distributors and is quite successful. He is so successful that he added to the size of his store last year by leasing the empty store next to his and expanding his store by 25%.

Key points from this chapter:

1. Inventory varies at different dollar stores but the categories are similar.
2. There are many different categories to choose from.
3. There are wholesalers and distributors who work directly with dollar stores.

Dollar Tree

Dollar Tree stores are a different type of dollar store. They are corporate owned, not the mom-and-pop-type stores that I love. However, Dollar Tree can definitely be a source of very profitable products to resell. One huge advantage that Dollar Tree shoppers (and resellers) have is that you can purchase from Dollar Tree online. DollarTree.com offers many of the items you can find in stores and provides free in-store pickup of your online purchases. You can also have the items sent directly to you.

Let's go back to the original idea of searching your local dollar store for items to resell. At Dollar Tree, when you find a profitable item, you can then purchase additional quantities from their website. If you are in their store, they have a tear-off sheet that you can use to re-order as well. I would suggest that you begin your search in the actual store. This will allow you to check the quality of an item.

Be careful! When you scan items, especially in the grocery section of Dollar Tree, be sure to note the quantity being sold in the listing. For example, I found a 3.5 oz box of Bumble Bee Hummus (Figure 11). When you see the listing, you must note that the selling price of $29.94 is for a pack of six boxes. You are NOT getting almost $30 for one little 3.5 ounce box. This is very important in all of your scanning, not just at dollar stores. However I do see this more often with grocery items. Go ahead and buy six of the boxes of hummus for $6. Your profit will still be $15.39.

Bumble Bee, Classic Hummus with Wheat Crackers, Ready to Eat, 3.5oz Box (Pack of 6)

from Bumble Bee
Be the first to review this item

Price: $29.94 ($4.99 / Item) *Prime*

Only 1 left in stock.
Sold by Cool Stuff and Fulfilled by Amazon. Gift-wrap available.

- Bumble Bee
- Classic Hummus
- with Wheat Crackers and Plastic Spreader
- 3.5oz Box
- Pack of 6

8 new from $29.94

Figure 11

From Dollar Tree's corporate website: Dollar Tree, a Fortune 500 Company, now operates more than 13,600 stores across 48 states and five Canadian provinces. Stores operate under the brands of Dollar Tree, Dollar Tree Canada, Deals and Family Dollar. Yes, Family

Dollar. Dollar Tree announced the acquisition of Family Dollar in July of 2015. It will be interesting to see how this affects the prices in Family Dollar.

With more than 13,600 Dollar Tree stores, I was curious to see how many are within 10 miles of my house. I live in northern New Jersey, which is full of retail stores, malls, strip malls and more. I will definitely run out of money and time before I ever run out of places to shop. There are five Dollar Tree stores and another 11 mom-and-pop dollar stores within 10 miles of my house. This makes sourcing for products at dollar stores very easy for me.

For those of you without a dollar store anywhere near you, hop online and do a little *Online Arbitrage* (buying products online to resell for a profit). Go to DollarTree.com and search the items there for profitable items to resell on Amazon. The added bonus is that you can shop anytime and have the items shipped directly to you. Remember to buy smaller quantities until you can verify the quality of the items and also to make sure that the items you have researched actually sell and give you the profit you expect. Once you find some winners, go deep. Buy deep (larger quantities) into products that sell well for you. There are a few more benefits to buying online at Dollar Tree. The site makes it easy to buy tax-exempt, provides recall information, has weekly ads, closeouts and new arrivals.

Key points from this chapter:

1. Dollar Tree is a different type of dollar store.
2. Take advantage of www.dollartree.com.
3. Buy small at first and then go deep on successful purchases.

What Can You Resell From a Dollar Store?

Here is the million dollar question: What should you buy to resell? I have already suggested that you should have the ability to scan products while shopping in a dollar store, but where do you begin? You walk into a store with eight aisles of merchandise and you don't know where to turn. I suggest that you start with something you know. If you have children, head over to the baby supplies or toys aisles. If you were in a home improvement store last weekend and know what the prices were like there, you will want to head to tools or housewares.

Let's start in the baby aisle. I can save you some time right away; don't bother with anything that is Baby King brand. Baby King is a dollar store–only brand and most buyers know it. You want to give people some value for their money while still making a profit yourself. Glance through the rows of baby merchandise and look for anything that you recognize as a superior brand. I recently found some Tommee Tippee pacifiers that I sold within a week for $12 each. The packaging itself can give it away, the Tommee Tippee pacifiers were not in a plastic bubble on cardboard backing. Instead, they were in a clear plastic carrying case wrapped with their information card. That type of item grabs your attention because your first thought is, "Wow, that's only a dollar?!"

"How can they be selling that for only a dollar?" This is the best indication that you may have found something worth scanning. Flip it over and scan the UPC. Is the item currently on Amazon? Is it selling for at least $10? Can you determine the sales rank? Remember that the lower the sales rank number, the better the sales of that item. If you find an item that sells for $10 or more and has a good sales rank, you definitely want to grab it. If the sales rank is 5000 or lower, you can feel confident in buying every one of that item that they have. Now, what is the brand of the item in your hand? Are there any other items on the rack that are the same brand or are similar in some other way? Scan those next.

This same strategy works in tools and housewares. In general the Tri-sonic brand is a dollar-store-only brand and you can skip it. What else looks good? If you know something about tools, you can look for sets that sell for at least $10 at a home improvement store. Is there something like that here? Remember, you are looking for an item that will provide value to your customer. I once found a tool set containing a level and a tape measure plus a carrying case for both that attached to your belt. I sold the set for $25. Unfortunately there was only one on the shelf and the store didn't have any more.

Let's wander over to electronics. Try to resist shopping for yourself. You do not need a $1 phone charger and neither does anyone else. These are a quick fix if you need to charge your phone in a pinch but they have no longevity. Spend your money on a brand-name charger for best results. Cell phone cases are another eye-catcher but they are up near the cash registers for a reason; they are impulse buys. When you are waiting in line, you pick up and play with the items near the counter and convince yourself that you really need that pink leopard print phone case or that camo print mouse pad. No you don't. Would you "need" it if it were $10? Would you search for it on Amazon if you hadn't already seen it? Probably not.

Look deeper into the electronics shelves and look for the items that look "too good for a dollar store." Scan anything that is for e-readers like Kindle or Nook. With the demise of local bookstores, e-readers are very popular but accessories for them are hard to find except online. I would have never thought to go to a dollar store to look for a case for my Kindle Keyboard but, lo and behold, there were 14 on the shelf. I admit, I kept one for myself. After scanning the barcode I discovered that, not only would these sell for more than $12 each, but the rank was below 100! That is unbelievable. I asked the owner if they had more and he checked the stockroom. He brought out a case which contained 24 more. I bought them all for $1 each. My payout was $8.24 on each one and they all sold within two weeks. Some quick math shows that 37 x $8.24=$304.88, minus my cost of $37 left me with a profit of $267.88 in two weeks!

Electronics is not limited to accessories for your electronic devices, so be sure to look for brand names that you recognize: Panasonic, Sony, GE, Phillips. If you don't know where to begin, flip over a few items and scan them. I recommend turning down the volume on the media setting of your phone so that you don't beep every time you scan an item. You may be mistaken for an employee and you don't want strangers walking up to you asking for your help. This is the same reason you should never wear a red shirt to a Target store, you blend in with the employees. Trust me, I know from personal experience.

There is one category in your local dollar store that you should look at very carefully and I would suggest scanning every product: *Regional items.* These are items, usually sports team merchandise, that are specific to your location. You may find a local dollar store that carries both pro sports and college items. Since I am in the New York/New Jersey metropolitan area, my favorite dollar store has a selection of NY Giants, NY Jets, NY Mets, NY Yankees and occasionally NJ Devils merchandise. Because the 2014 Super Bowl was played here at the Meadowlands, I was able to get NFL Super Bowl totes for $1 each (Figure 12). They are certainly not as popular now, but they were great in February!

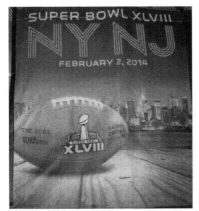

NFL Super Bowl XLVIII (48) New York New Jersey
Football Reusable Grocery Tote Bag Large
by NFL
Be the first to review this item

Currently unavailable.
We don't know when or if this item will be back in stock.

- Large Super Bowl reusable tote 12.5" x 13.5" x 8" deep
- Celebrating Super Bowl XLVIII at the Meadowlands in NJ
- Football with NY Skyline design
- Perfect as a large gift bag for the football fan
- Official NFL product

Figure 12

Scan every item in the Regional section and, when you get home do a little additional searching to see if anyone has created **bundles** or sets of these items. **Bundles** are discussed in more detail when I talk about creating your own listings. They are basically sets of similar items sold on Amazon as a "bundle." Just remember to check out those regional items, there are plenty of fans that live outside of their team's region. For example, my husband is a Dallas fan and I am a Patriot's fan, so online purchasing is the only way to go. One possible exception to this rule is NASCAR merchandise (Figure 13). It absolutely sells well but be careful because a driver's number can change and people prefer their driver's current car number reflected in their fan gear.

#24 Jeff Gordon 3x5 Flag

★★★☆☆ ▾ 6 customer reviews

List Price: ~~$19.99~~
Price: $15.99 + $5.99 shipping
You Save: $4.00 (20%)

Note: Not eligible for Amazon Prime.

In Stock.

- 3'x5' Outdoor Flag
- Single Sided - Reverse (mirror image) shows through to back
- Has grommets for attaching to standard flagpole
- Officially Licensed

Figure 13

I have given you a few ideas of places to start your search in your local dollar store. Don't limit yourself to the brands I have discussed.

Key points from this chapter:

1. Look for items that don't look like they belong in a dollar store.
2. Start in an aisle of the store that is familiar to you.
3. Look for brand names that you recognize.
4. Once you find a winner, look for more items similar to that one, either the same brand or some variation of the item you have found.
5. Ask an employee if there are more in the back.

What Shouldn't You Resell From a Dollar Store?

Toilet paper. Don't use it and don't try to resell it. The quality is poor and there is no reason to waste your time. Life's too short to use lousy toilet paper. But seriously, as I previously mentioned, Amazon has outlined items that are prohibited or restricted for sale on their website. (Toilet paper is neither prohibited nor restricted.) It is your responsibility to be aware of the rules on Amazon and sell accordingly. If you are not approved to sell in a specific category, don't try to work around it. There is plenty of great merchandise to sell and no reason to jeopardize your ability to sell on Amazon.

When you use the Amazon app to scan merchandise, it immediately lets you know if you are eligible to sell that item. I am not approved to sell clothing so I don't even bother looking at the socks, scarves and other clothing items that can be found in a dollar store. The only exception to this would be an item that is considered sporting goods, like knee pads or exercise gloves. The

ScanPower app will display the category of an item but the Amazon app wins this round with the clear decision of whether or not you're are allowed to sell the specific item.

There are also some items that are simply not a good idea to sell on Amazon. Recent news articles report that some dog treats made in China caused illness, injury and even death in dogs. Selling edible dog treats including rawhides that are made in China is a bad idea. Similarly, pay close attention to children's toys. Knock–off brands can be harmful to children. Toys with small parts should have choking warnings on them, and most toys should have a recommended age on the package.

A final category that I avoid is glassware. You are welcome to sell glassware but it requires so much additional preparation that it is often not worth your time and the cost of materials. This is a perfect example of knowing Amazon's policy on the items you want to sell. Amazon's Packaging and Prep Requirements for glassware and breakables can be found here: https://www.amazon.com/gp/help/customer/display.html/ref=hp_rel_topic?ie=UTF8&nodeId=200280450.

According to Amazon's Requirements: "Fragile Units should be packaged so they will not break and possibly create a safety hazard during storage, shipment preparation, or shipment to the customer. A fragile Unit must be packaged in either a six solid-sided box, or completely secured in bubble wrap, so the Unit is not exposed in any way (Figure 14). Individually wrap or box all units to prevent damage. For example, in a set of four wine glasses, each individual wine glass must be wrapped. Wrap multiple Units individually to prevent them from damaging one another within their package." See Figure 14 for Amazon's example of correct packaging for fragile items

Make sure your packaged Units can pass a 3-foot drop test onto a hard surface without breaking. An Amazon drop test consists of five drops:

- Flat on base
- Flat on top
- Flat on longest side
- Flat on shortest side
- On a corner

Not permitted:
The Unit is exposed and unprotected.
Parts can snag and break.

Permitted: The Unit is protected
with bubble wrap preventing
parts from snagging.

Figure 14

You can see why I avoid breakables in general. You are
permitted to sell this type of item, just be sure to follow
Amazon's rules.

It's important for you to be aware of all of the rules
regarding the categories in which you want to sell. If you
sell plush toys or items such as stuffed toys, animals,
and puppets, you must package them so they will not be

damaged during receipt, stocking, shipment preparation, or shipment to the customer. These units must be placed in a sealed poly bag or shrink-wrapped. This includes units in an open box that is not completely sealed (Figure 15).

Examples of prepped units

Not permitted: The Unit is in an open box that is not sealed.

Permitted: The Unit is enclosed in sealed box and the open faced is sealed. See poly bag requirements in the Packaging Requirements section.

Figure 15

Amazon's policy on poly-bagged units can be found here:
https://www.amazon.com/gp/help/customer/display.html/ref=help_search_1-1?ie=UTF8&nodeId=200243250&qid=1438046876&sr=1-1#poly

Here are some of the highlights of Amazon's policy on poly-bagged Units.

Poly bags used to protect units must meet the following requirements: Poly bags with a 5" opening or larger (measured when flat) are required to have a suffocation warning, either printed on the bag itself or attached as a label. For example: "WARNING: To avoid danger of suffocation, keep this plastic bag away from babies and children. Do not use this bag in cribs, beds, carriages or play pens. This bag is not a toy."

This warning should be in a prominent location and in a legible font size for the size of the bag. The thickness of the bag must be at least 1.5 mils. The poly bag must be transparent. The barcode label must be scannable through the bag or be placed on the outside of the bag. Poly bags must be completely sealed. Poly bag or shrink wrap must not protrude more than 3 inches past the dimensions of the product.

Take a good look at Amazon's Hazardous Materials Policy.
https://sellercentral.amazon.com/gp/help/201003400/ref=sm_201003400_cont_201003420

Amazon has recently updated their HAZMAT policies so be sure to keep up to date on them. Before listing products for Fulfillment by Amazon, it's important to know which products are suitable for the fulfillment process and which are not. Most products that are regulated as a hazardous material by the U.S. Department of Transportation (DOT) cannot be processed by Amazon's fulfillment centers. This includes, but is not limited to:

Explosives

Flammable liquids or solids

Poisons

Lithium ion and lithium metal batteries, or products containing those   batteries either within or with the main product

Once again, know the rules of the categories in which you wish to sell. I cannot stress this point enough. At a minimum, Amazon will remove your items and dispose of them without reimbursement, but you could also be subject to suspension from Amazon, so be aware of the rules.

You can generally sell food items on Amazon, if they are pre-packaged and have expiration dates greater than **90 days** from the time Amazon receives them. If you find food at a dollar store that should have an expiration date but doesn't, leave it on the shelf. It is not worth any possible problems. Be sure to read Amazon's policies on food items as well as their complete rules pertaining to expiration dates and meltables. FBA accepts products that are subject to melting (such as chocolates) only between October 1 and April 30 of each calendar year. Amazon has a strict policy on items that will melt in the summer. These items can be merchant fulfilled but they cannot be stored in the Amazon fulfillment centers.

Key points from this chapter:

1. If you are not approved to sell in a specific category, don't try to work around that fact. Either try to get approved or sell something else.
2. Avoid selling any items that could be a safety issue.
3. Know the Amazon rules for the categories in which you want to sell.

Creating a New Listing

Let's go back to the earlier example of the Mickey Mouse toy that you found in the dollar store (Figure 1). Perhaps he was sitting in a bin with other Disney characters. Since he was a good purchase, perhaps his bin mates are good deals too. You scan the UPC on Minnie Mouse and discover that she is selling for $10.10. Next you scan Pluto and he is selling for $14.98! You can't get the plush into your basket fast enough. But then you scan Donald Duck and there is no listing. The same happens for Daisy Duck and Goofy. Now what? I suggest that you first attempt to search by the title, similar to Mickey Mouse's. "Disney 9 Inch Plush Goofy." "Disney Plush Donald Duck." "Disney Plush Daisy Duck." But let's suppose that those three remain elusive. Should you buy them or not?

I would suggest that you buy at least one of each. You would only be spending and additional $3 and it would give you the opportunity to do more research at home. Since the other three characters are selling well, it is likely that Donald, Daisy and Goofy will also sell. Sometimes the "other" characters, those secondary characters that are harder to find, result in good profits. The Pluto plush toy is a great example of this at $14.98.

There is a lot of detailed information on the next few pages, so take it slow and re-read it as often as needed. Once you have created your first listing, the next ones are MUCH easier, I promise. Creating a new product page is not difficult and Amazon's Help Pages give you the information you need to do so accurately. You need a Pro Merchant account to create a new listing page. You can create product detail pages for products not available in the Amazon.com catalog using the Add a Product or bulk upload tools in your seller account.

When you create a product detail page, you agree to follow certain rules and restrictions. Amazon provides a complete list of these here: https://www.amazon.com/gp/help/customer/display.html/ref=help_search_1-1?ie=UTF8&nodeId=10683361&qid=1438047277&sr=1-1

Here are two important rules to note: 1) Detail pages may not feature or contain Restricted Products. 2) All products listed on Amazon.com must meet North America product safety standards and Choking Hazard Warning Requirements (CPSIA).

When creating a listing or when matching an item to an existing listing, sellers must follow Amazon's listing standards for any product sold on Amazon.com. In other words, Amazon wants all of the listings on their site to meet their standards, including any applicable category-specific guidelines.

Now how do you actually create a listing? You need three main things to create a listing:

- the actual product

- a photo of the product

- the product's UPC.

So let's create a listing for our Goofy plush toy. First, we need a photo worthy of an Amazon listing. As usual, Amazon has rules for its pictures too. Every product on Amazon needs one or more product images. The primary image of your item is called the "MAIN." The MAIN image represents an item in search results and browse pages and is the first image customers see on an item's detail page. Choose images that are clear, easy to understand, information-rich, and attractively presented. Images must accurately represent the product and show only the product that's for sale, with minimal or no propping. Images are very important to customers, so quality matters.

MAIN images must show the actual product (not a graphic, drawing or illustration) and must NOT show excluded accessories, props that may confuse the customer, text that is not part of the product, or logos/watermarks/inset images. The product must fill 85% or more of the image. Images should be 1000 pixels or larger in either height or width, to enable zoom function on the website (zoom has proven to enhance sales). The smallest your file should be is 500 pixels on the longest side. Amazon accepts JPEG (.jpg), TIFF (.tif), or GIF (.gif) file formats. JPEG is preferred.

Figure 16

Here is your photo of Goofy as a jpeg (Figure 16).

Now let's get him listed. You always want to make sure you search Amazon for your item first. You do not want to create a duplicate listing because this is against Amazon policy.

Since you already looked for your Goofy plush toy and found no listing, you can now click "Create a new product" on Seller Central>Inventory>Add a Product page (Figure 17).

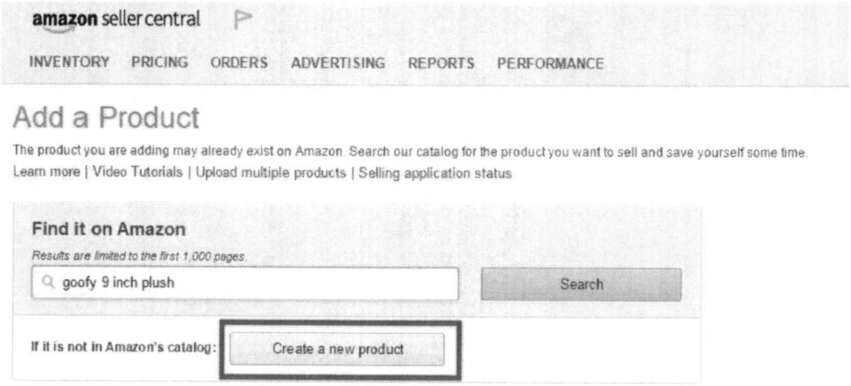

Figure 17

First you need to classify your product by selecting the most appropriate category for your item (Figure 18). All products should be appropriately and accurately classified to the most specific location available. Incorrectly classifying products is prohibited. Remember, you can only create listings for items in categories for which you are already approved. For example, if you want to list a watch, you cannot list it if you are not approved to sell watches. Selecting a different category for that watch to "sneak it in" is the fastest way to get banned from selling on Amazon. The toy category is open so Goofy is safe to list.

You can type in a few words about Goofy (Goofy 9 inch Plush), click "Find Category" and Amazon will suggest the most likely main category for your item, in this case "Toys & Games" (Figure 18).

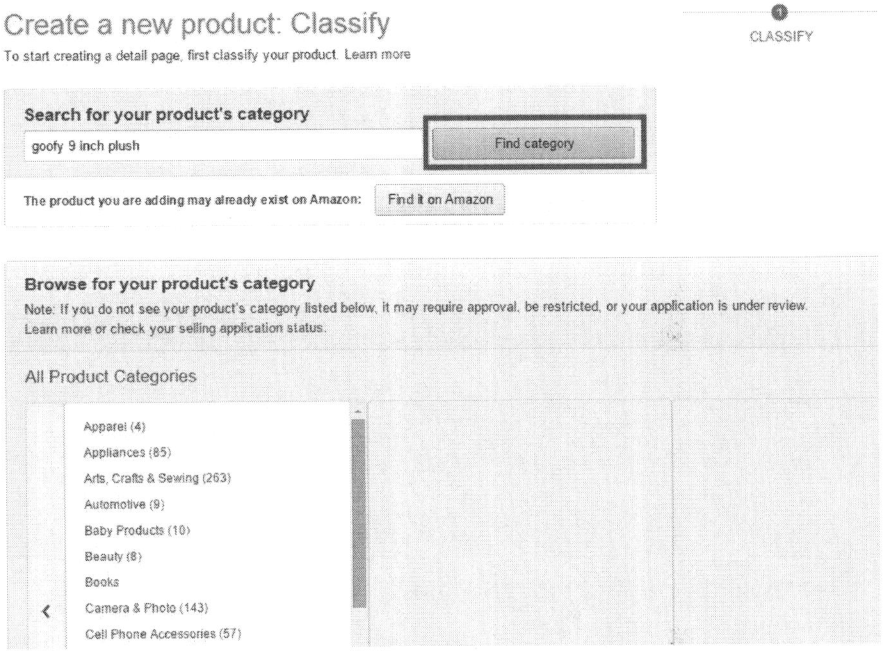

Figure 18

You will then select a subcategory. You can see in Figure 19 that the most appropriate choice is Stuffed Toys>Plush Toys>Other Plush Toys since Goofy is not a puppet, backpack nor pillow which are your other choices. Clearly he is not an automotive part, either.

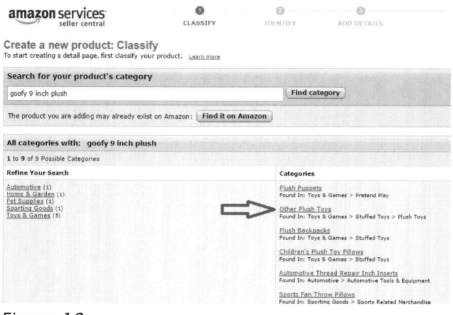

Figure 19

Once you click "Other Plush Toys," you are ready to create your product detail page. When creating a product detail page, provide only information that pertains to the features of the product in general, **NOT** the condition of your particular item. Product detail pages may be used by any other seller to list the same product. There are six tabs along the top of Amazon's Create a New Product listing page. This is what Amazon refers to as the "offer listing pipeline." The offer listing pipeline provides an opportunity to note the item's condition, quantity, price, and other seller-specific details that are relevant to a specific listing. We will visit and complete each one in order.

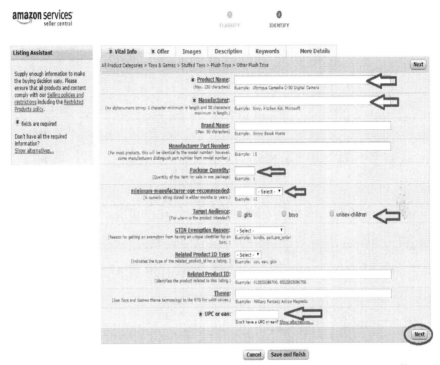

Figure 20

On the first tab, you will enter the "Vital Info" about your product (Figure 20). Your title is the "Product Name" and should read "Disney Goofy 9 Inch Plush" and not "New Goofy toy with bent tag, adorable!" Stick to the facts about the item in general.

Continue to fill in the form including all lines marked with an asterisk (*). I highly recommend filling in all fields for which you have the accurate information, including package quantity. In this example, you are selling one Goofy toy even though you may have six available to sell. For items in the toy category, you must also include the "minimum-manufacturer-age-recommended" (from the item's tag or packaging) and the Target Audience (often "unisex"). Although these fields are not marked with an asterisk, you will eventually get an error message if you skip them. Finally, enter the UPC from the item itself. Be sure to fill in all fields that correspond with those that I have marked with an arrow in Figure 20.

Be aware that sometimes similar items will have the same UPC barcode number. A good example of this is small die-cast cars. Multiple cars will have the same UPC although they are entirely different cars. For example, the UPC 0027084984224 returns results of '71 El Camino; Cadillac CTS-V; Muscle Mania Ford Thunderbolt PINK; Showroom Nissan Titan; and Mars Rover Curiosity. In that situation, you would create variations for the item. The Create a Product listing page offers sellers the option to create variations of products in certain categories. See Amazon's help pages for complete instructions on creating listings with variations. https://www.amazon.com/gp/help/customer/display.html/ref=help_search_1-1?ie=UTF8&nodeId=200783950&qid=1438049595&sr=1-1

Once you enter all of the Vital Info about your item, click "Next." DO NOT CLICK "Save and Finish!" When you click "Next" at the bottom of the page, you will then enter your "Offer" information (Figure 21). This page relates specifically to YOUR item. This is where you add the condition of YOUR item, any condition notes (such as a bent tag) as well as the price you set for YOUR item. I hope I have made it clear that this is the only page in this listing creation process that specifically relates to the product YOU have in your hand.

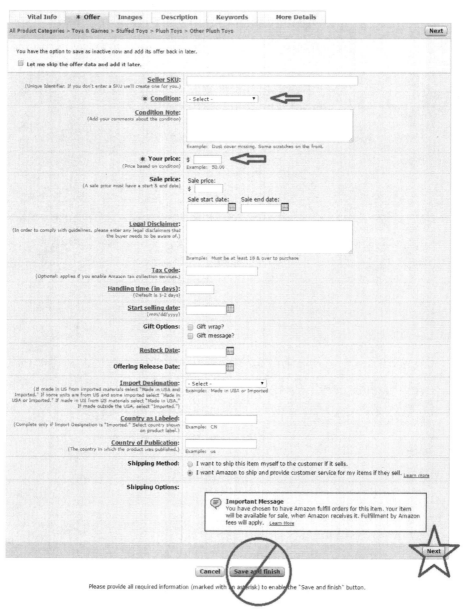

Figure 21

Again, you must click "Next," **NOT** "Save and Finish." If you click the pretty gold "Save and Finish" button you will get error messages from Amazon that your listing is incomplete, you are missing images, key information and details. Clicking "Next" will take you to the "Images" tab (Figure 22).

Figure 22

As per Amazon, MAIN images must have a pure white background. Pure white blends in with the Amazon search and item detail pages – RGB values of 255, 255, 255. *RGB* (red, green, and blue) refers to a system for representing the colors to be used on a computer display. I use the free website www.fotofuse.com to create a pure white background. Take a photo of your item on a plain white background. You can use any device (camera, iPad, smartphone) that you like to take the photo. I prefer to use my cellphone and upload the photo directly to my computer. From there, I open the Fotofuse website and follow their directions to fix the background of the photo. You can fix your background with whatever tools you like, this is just my preferred option.

Click "Choose File" under MAIN, find the file on your computer (the one with the correct pure white background) and click "open." Your image will appear in place of the gray camera icon (Figure 23). Additional images can then be added. You may wonder how many pictures are necessary for your item. Think about it from the perspective of a customer. A plush toy really only needs one photo unless there is a special design on the back. On the other hand, an electronic item, a small set of items or an intricate item with small details would need more pictures for someone to make an informed buying decision. I always suggest taking a picture as if there is no description because the photo really sells the item.

Upload your jpeg of Goofy into the MAIN image of the Images tab.

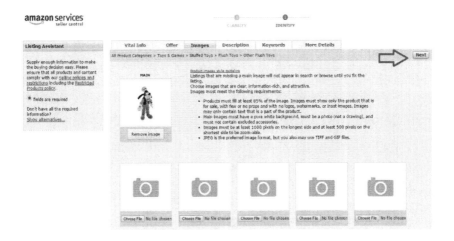

Figure 23

Click "Next" at the top or bottom of the screen to go to the "Description" tab.

Figure 24

This is where you add the information that appears as bullet points next to the image of your product (Figure 24). You will also provide the Product Description which is found farther down the page of the Amazon listing.

Product titles, product descriptions and bullets must be clearly written and should assist the customer in understanding the product. These attributes should comply with the category-specific style guide recommendations. The bullet points that you enter in the "Key Product Features" section of this tab are based on the item in general, not the condition of the one you have for sale. Enter each product feature as a sentence fragment with no period at the end. Be factual and brief but be sure to include key features such as size, color and other important attributes. See an example in Figure 25. Always proofread what you have written. You do not want embarrassing misspellings for all to see.

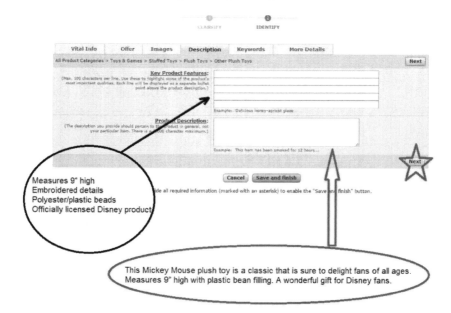

Figure 25

On the "Descriptions" tab you will enter the information that the buyer sees for the product. Figure 25 shows an example of what you should include in your "Key Product Features" and "Product Description" fields. Remember to keep these points brief and factual. Even Amazon shoppers who are browsing on their phone or similar digital device will immediately see these attributes for your product. Help the shopper by providing a fast glimpse of the most important features.

Amazon policy prohibits the use of information about the seller in product descriptions so avoid phrases like "see my other listings" or "sold by me." Include only information about the product for sale.

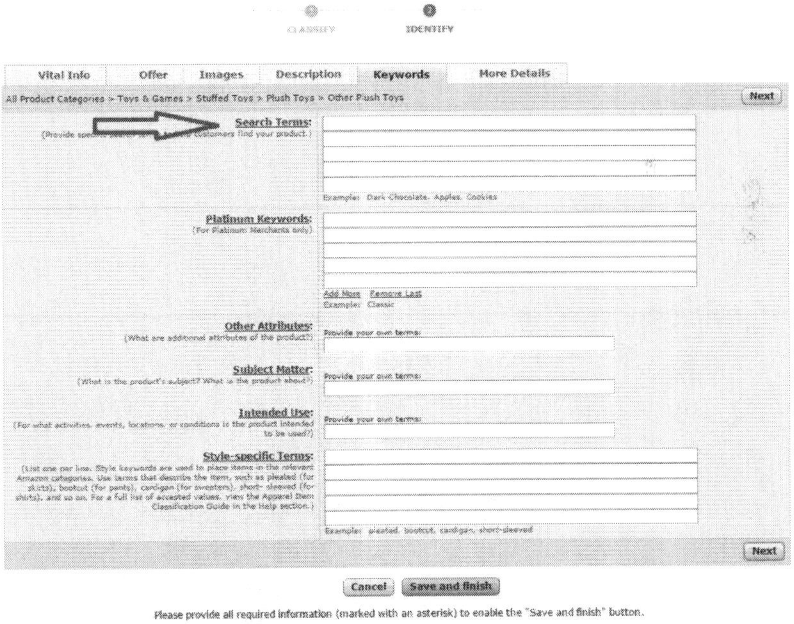

Figure 26

Click "Next" to go to the next page where you will enter keywords for your item (Figure 26). The search terms you provide will help shoppers find your item. These do not appear anywhere on the Amazon product listing page. Keep your keywords relevant to the item, but there is no need to add words that are already in the title. Possible keywords for Goofy might be Playhouse Disney, cartoon, Mickey Mouse pal, dog, stuffed animal, bean bag or toy. I often do a Google search on an item that I don't know very much about to find appropriate search terms.

Amazon prohibits the use of HTML, DHTML, Java, scripts, or other types of executables in your detail pages. The use of false product identification information, including UPC codes, in product detail pages is also prohibited.

Your final "Next" click will bring you to the "More Details" tab (Figure 27). This screen is a very large and intimidating page but you only need to enter information that applies to your item. Skip any fields that do not apply to your listing and **do not** enter "N/A" anywhere. You must fill in the dimensions of the actual item, its weight and the item's package dimensions and shipping weight. Do not enter the Manufacturer's Suggested Retail Price unless you know it. Also include the color and material type. The tush-tag of a toy will have the material type. The color may just be "multi" unless it is obviously a solid color (e.g. Red M&M toy).

The product dimensions and the package dimensions may be the same but often they are different. Consider a small toy that is 2 x 1 x 1 inches packaged in a plastic bubble on a card that a store can hang on a peg hook. The card is actually 4 x 3 x 1.5 inches. It is important to accurately measure your item because FBA storage fees are charged for all units stored in an Amazon fulfillment center based on calendar month and your daily average volume (measured in cubic feet). The cubic feet of any unit will be based on the unit's size including its packaging, in this case 4 x 3 x 1.5 inches. More information on all fees associated with FBA are on Amazon.com.

Vital Info	Offer	Images	Description	Keywords	More Details

All Product Categories > Toys & Games > Stuffed Toys > Plush Toys > Other Plush Toys   **Next**

Manufacturer's Suggested Retail Price: $ [____]
(Manufacturer's suggested retail price (MSRP)--not the price for which you plan to sell it. Don't know the MSRP? Leave it blank.)   Example: 49.99

Is Discontinued by Manufacturer: ☐
(Is this item no longer produced by the manufacturer?)   Example: true

Product Dimensions: Length: [____] Height: [____] Width: [____] - Select - ▼ ⇐
(The dimensions and weight of the product itself, without its packaging.)
Weight: [____] - Select - ▼ ⇐

Shipping Weight: - Select - ▼ ⇐
(Weight of the product when packaged to ship)   Example: 2.0

Color: [_____] ⇐
(The color of the item.)   Example: Red, Navy Blue, Pink, Green

Size: [_____] ⇐
(The numeric or text version of the item's size.)   Example: 2T, 6X, 12, Small, X-Large, 18 months, 14 Tall, 28Wx32L

Is Recalled?: ☐
(Indicate if the product has been recalled.)   Example: true

Is Assembly Required: ☐
(Indicate if assembly is required.)   Example: false

Assembly Time: - Select - ▼
(Time to completely assemble product.)   Example: 20 Minutes

Assembly Instructions: [_____]
(Instructions to assemble product.)   Example: Insert piece A into the upper pre-drilled holes on piece B.

Number of Pieces: [____]
(Number of pieces)   Example: 1250

Package Dimensions: Length: [____] Height: [____] Width: [____] - Select - ▼ ⇐
(The dimensions and weight of the product in the manufacturer's original packaging.)
Weight: [____] - Select - ▼

Material Type: [_____]
(What material is the product made out of?) [_____]
[_____]
[_____]
Add More   Remove Last
Example: nylon, wood, steel

Fabric Type: [_____]
(List all fabrics, separated by /, and % of each from most to least. Always add "viscose" or "rayon" if listing bamboo, and "azlon" if listing soy. Click "Fabric Type" for an example.) [_____]
Example: 90% cotton/10% rayon

Department: [_____]
(Select a value from the list of Valid Values.) [_____]
[_____]
[_____]
[_____]
Example: womens

Max Aggregate Ship Quantity: [____]
(A positive integer.)   Example: 0, 100, or 12142

Batteries are Included: ☐
(Indicate if batteries are included with the product.)   Example: true

Next

Cancel   **Save and finish**

Please provide all required information (marked with an asterisk) to enable the "Save and finish" button.

Figure 27

Now I will finally let you click that gold "Save and finish" button (Figure 27). From there you are on the page where you "Create or Add to an Existing Shipping Plan" just as if you were adding into your inventory an item that already had a listing on Amazon, because now it does! You have officially created a new listing. You did it!

Please note that Amazon may change the appearance of the Create a New Product listing pages but the listing creation process is still the same.

Key points from this chapter:

1. Only create a new listing if you are sure your product isn't already on Amazon.
2. Know the rules.
3. Follow the tabs on Amazon's Create a New Product listing page.

Create a Bundle

There is another option for making money on products from your favorite dollar store. Create a bundle. A bundle is simply a group of items sold together in a set as one item. According to Amazon policy, a bundle "must consist of items that are highly complementary and provide a value to the buyer when compared to the individual items purchased separately." All products in bundles must comply with Amazon's Product Listing Policies.

Let's go back to the earlier example of the Mickey Mouse toy that you found in a bin with other Disney characters. Since Mickey was a good purchase, you searched further and found that Minnie and Pluto were selling well too. Then you found Donald Duck, Daisy Duck and Goofy, who were not even listed. Your option was to list the three plush that were already in Amazon's catalog (Mickey, Minnie and Pluto) and then to create a listing for each of the other three toys (Donald, Daisy and Goofy).

You have just seen how to create a new listing. Now you can use that same procedure for listing a bundle of items. You could sell Mickey for $10, Minnie for $11 and Pluto for $14 for a total profit of $18.68 after Amazon fees for each individual listing or you could take all three of these plush and put them in a bundle (Figure 28). You would still charge the same combined price of $35. However, because it is only one listing, your fees are lower and your total profit is now $22.06!

Figure 28

This gives you a great opportunity for the Donald Duck, Daisy Duck and Goofy you have who were not even listed before. Instead of creating three separate listings, you can create one listing for these three items (Figure 29).

Figure 29

Yes, you can absolutely list these three toys as separate listings and sell them individually until you are completely sold out. I am just offering an alternative that will allow you to make more money with less work. If you choose this route, you will want to make sure you have the same number of each of these plush toys. In other words, once you create a bundle, every bundle you sell under that Amazon listing must contain the exact same three items. If you want to sell five of these bundles, you must buy five each of Donald, Daisy and Goofy. When you ship these toys into Amazon's warehouse, you will package all three of these together to sell as a set/bundle.

One question you may ask is, "What should I bundle?"
Amazon answers this question for you. When you are
looking at a listing on Amazon, scroll to the bottom
where Amazon suggests other items for sale:
"Frequently Bought Together" and "Customers Who
Bought This Item Also Bought." A perfect example is at
the bottom of the listing for your Mickey Mouse plush
toy (Figure 30).

Frequently Bought Together

Price for all three: $34.53

Add all three to Cart

Add all three to Wish List

Show availability and shipping details

☑ **This item:** Disney Mickey Mouse Mini Bean Bag Plush $9.45

☑ Disney Minnie Mouse Plush - Red Mini Bean Bag - 9 1/4" $10.10

☑ Disney Pluto 9" Plush Bean Bag Dog $14.98

Figure 30

You can see how this bundle could be profitable.
Shoppers are already purchasing these three toys
together. If you create a bundle that contains all three of
these toys, you could then charge $35, which also
means you customers qualify for free shipping. More
value for the customer, more money for you and less
work on your part. This is a triple win for you. It follows
Amazon's bundle rules of including items that are highly

complementary and provide a value to the buyer when compared to the individual items purchased separately.

Let's look at a different possibility for a bundle with your original Mickey Mouse toy. You could create a Mickey Back-to-School bundle, a Mickey Easter Basket bundle or a Mickey Travel bundle. Just think, the family is packing for a trip to Disney World and mom packs a set of toys to keep her child happy during the trip. Maybe Mom bought a bundle like the one in Figure 31. It includes a Mickey Mouse plush, a water bottle, stickers, a puzzle to color and colored pencils in a Mickey Mouse theme.

Figure 31

This bundle could easily be used in an Easter basket, as a birthday gift or for a back-to-school set. Well-designed product bundles provide convenience and value to buyers. Adhere to Amazon's bundling policy and the following guidelines for their creation. This will help Amazon customers locate specific bundles more easily, and prevent duplicate listings.

Sellers can create bundles composed of different products to create a new bundled product. Bundled products may be listed in all categories except Books,

Music, Video, and DVD (collectively, BMVD) and Video Games. Bundles are only allowed when the primary product in the bundle is not a BMVD or Video Games product. For example, you can list a bundle composed of a yoga mat (the primary product), a yoga DVD and a yoga book, but you cannot list a bundle composed of only a yoga DVD and a yoga book because both are BMVD. In this case, list each item separately.

According to Amazon's policy, all bundles are subject to review for appropriateness and relevance. Amazon will determine whether a bundle complies with this policy. Failure to adhere to the policy may result in the removal, without notice, of any bundled product listing, account suspension, or both. A bundle may only be listed in a single category, even if the products within the bundle are from multiple categories. If a bundle does include products from multiple categories the bundle may only be listed in the single category to which the highest priced item in the bundle best relates, excluding any BMVD or Video Games product, even if it is the highest priced item in the bundle. Also, a bundle cannot contain any separate warranty products or extended service plans.

Furthermore, Amazon requires that bundle images, features and descriptions must adhere to all of Amazon's listing policies. For example, as with single products, information about the seller is not allowed in product descriptions. Include only information about the products in the bundle.

Each bundle must have its own unique identifier. In other words, the UPC of any individual product in the bundle may not serve as the UPC for the bundle. You are responsible for obtaining a new UPC for each bundle you create. NOTE: Use of the UPC from any single product in the bundle to identify the entire bundle may lead to immediate removal of the bundle listing.

Did you know that you can buy a UPC? This opens up an incredible amount of possibilities. Not only will buying your own UPC allow you to create any bundle you want, it also allows you to create Amazon listings for items that do not have their own unique UPC/barcode. You can search online for websites that sell UPCs. I actually buy mine on eBay from "leadingedgecodes" for less than 2 cents each. You can also take a look at the following websites to compare prices and features.

www.cheap-upc-barcode.com

www.singleupc.com

www.qualityupc.com

It is important to know when a bundle is not considered a bundle. If the bundle is actually a multi-pack of the same product, then you cannot list it as a bundle. In this case, use the options for displaying items with different package quantities. For example, Figure 32 shows a multi-pack of three sets of 20 batteries. This is a multi-pack, not a bundle.

Figure 32

Once you create a bundle, you may not modify the components of the bundle. Similarly, if you match your bundle to an existing bundle listing, the products in your bundle must be exactly the same as the products in the existing bundle in every respect. You may not change the components of the bundle listing. If your bundle is different in any way, you must create a new bundle listing instead of matching to the existing bundle. If you want to add or remove products from a bundle you created, you must remove the listing and create a new bundle listing with a unique UPC, or match to an existing bundle listing that is identical to your revised bundle. The detail pages for removed bundles may or may not remain on the website for other sellers to list against.

Amazon's Bundle Listing Content policy rules help maintain consistency throughout its listings. Include the word "Bundle" and the number of items in the bundle in the product title. Example title: *Lunch Tote Cooler Bag With Matching Tumbler and Freezer Pack Bundle 3 Items (Blue).* The first feature bullet must state that the product is a bundle of "X" number of items and include identification of the products in the bundle. The description must also state that the product is a bundle and identify the specific products included in the bundle (with appropriate designators such as model number, color and size).

Here is an example:

Lunch Tote Cooler Bag With Matching Tumbler and Freezer Pack Bundle 3 Items (Blue)

- Freezer pack keeps lunch cool in this pretty blue lunch tote with matching tumbler – Bundle of 3 Items
- 16 ounce Tumbler fits in the bag with room for the ice pack and other items.
- Lunch Bag is made of neoprene wetsuit fabric.
- Lead and PVC free. Velcro closure, tote measures 13" x 12" x 7"
- Stain resistant and machine washable in cold water. Drip dry. Very durable fabric with reinforced stitching.

Of course, Amazon's rules pertain to the photos as well. The main image for the bundle must include all of the exact products in the bundle, and **only** the products in the bundle. Images of representative products are not permitted. Follow all of Amazon's general rules for photos when creating listings for bundles.

Key points from this chapter:

1. All products in bundles must comply with Amazon's Product Listing Policies.

2. Look at items "Frequently Bought Together" and "Customers Who Bought This Item Also Bought" for bundle ideas.

3. Create bundles that offer value to the customer.

4. Know the difference between a multi-pack and a bundle.

Mini Bundles

Not to be confused with bundles of miniature items, "Mini Bundles" are small bundles of just two or three items. Larger bundles are profitable and as previously stated, provide more value for the customer, more money for you and less work on your part. There is one downside to a bundle of many individual items. What if you cannot find every single item? Remember, you may not change the components of the bundle listing, each bundle must contain the exact same items. Here is an example. The set shown in Figure 33 costs $9 at the dollar store as there are nine individual items. A package of 3 Hanging Paper Lanterns, 1 Candle, a package of 3 Hanging Danglers, a pack of 8 Dinner Plates, a pack of 16 Luncheon Napkins, a pack of 8 Paper Cups, a package of 8 Thank You Notes with Seals, a package of 4 Cut-outs and 1 Centerpiece.

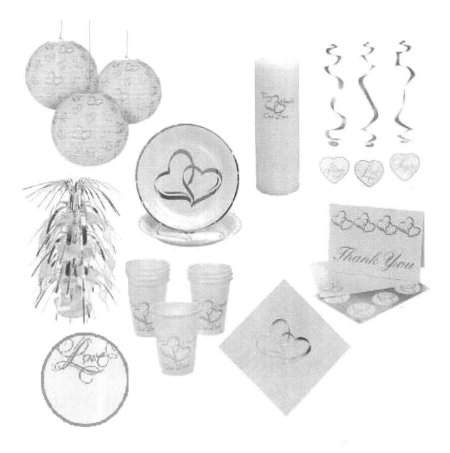

Figure 33

Now here is the problem: Let's say you can create this bundle and you can find four complete bundles to sell for $45 each. The next time you go to the store to replenish this set, there are no more candles. You can buy an additional six bundles without the candle but now you have to create a new listing for this different bundle. For the profit, it may be worth creating a new listing that could sell for $42. What if you go back to the store after those sell out and now you can only find four of the pieces of the set? Do you create yet another new bundle?

This is why I sometimes suggest what I call mini bundles. If you begin the process by creating a few different smaller bundles. Then if you cannot find one product, your other listings are still being profitable. The best mini bundles in this particular example would be: plates and napkins; the two sets of hanging décor; the centerpiece and cut–outs; and then the candle would probably sell well alone. You will be creating four bundles/listings at the very beginning, but it is much easier to replenish these smaller bundles than to try to replenish larger bundles and hope you can get all nine pieces later on. I speak from experience.

The key to listing these mini bundles is using extremely similar titles so that Amazon shoppers can find everything they need. For example, I would use the following titles:

- *Two Hearts Silver and White Love Wedding 8 Plates and 16 Napkins; (Figure 34)*

- *Two Hearts Silver and White Love Wedding 2 Sets of Hanging Décor 3 Round Lanterns 3 Dangling Hearts;*
- *Two Hearts Silver and White Love Wedding Centerpiece and 4 Cut-outs;*
- *Two Hearts Silver and White Love Wedding 10 Inch Unity.*

By repeating "**Two Hearts Silver and White Love Wedding**" in every title it will be simple for a buyer to find every matching listing.

Figure 34

I have found that some smaller bundles will actually sell faster because people have different needs and different tastes. A buyer may want just plates and napkins, while another wants balloons and décor. I like bundles that pair a set of paper party plates with matching napkins. Generally, plates are sold in a package of 8 and napkins in a set of 16. Customers will buy one pair if that is all they need, but they may need multiple pairs and will purchase three or four of your sets. The additional bonus for you is that your Amazon fees are slightly lower when people buy multiples of a product from you all at once. The Amazon buyer who needs place settings for 40 people may not need more than one set of décor. The matching titles allow customers to buy just what they need and the smaller bundles make it easier for you to replenish your inventory.

Key points from this chapter:

1. All products in bundles must comply with Amazon's Product Listing Policies.
2. Create smaller bundles using extremely similar titles.

Calendar of Profits

When considering the best time of year to turn a profit, neither brick-and-mortar retailers nor online sellers keep a straight January through December calendar. This is good for you because it means there is always an opportunity to make money. The 4th quarter of the calendar year (October, November and December) is traditionally the strongest time for retail sales. Retailers usually operate at a financial loss ("in the red") from January through November, and "Black Friday" (the day following Thanksgiving) indicates the point at which retailers begin to turn a profit (are "in the black"). This marks October through December as the most profitable time in retail. But online, especially on Amazon, sales begin to pick up as early as August and continue for at least a week into January as people redeem their gift cards after the holidays and buy themselves what they really wanted.

So let's take a look at what products you should be sending to Amazon and when. Consider the time it takes you to purchase items, prepare them for shipping to Amazon and actually ship them to the FBA warehouses.

Those items then need to be received at the warehouses and only then will they be available for customers to purchase. This is why I recommend buying your dollar store finds before you need them (especially themed merchandise) and certainly buy quickly when you see quality items that you can resell.

JANUARY is a good time to look toward Valentine's Day sales: gift baskets, roses, hearts, plush and candy. Anything "I love..." is popular at this time of year, including "I Love Grandma," "I Love Mom," "I Love Dad," I Love My Sister," and of course "I Love You" merchandise. This is a fabulous bundling opportunity. Adding a lovely container will make it a complete gift. The entire bundle should be well packaged to prevent damage in shipping to and from Amazon. Send Valentine's Day gift items and candy early in the month. You want it all to be received by Amazon and ready to sell right up to the second week of February. Last minute shoppers will order from Amazon and happily pay extra for overnight shipping if necessary. Hell hath no fury like a woman whose man forgot Valentine's Day.

For a young girl
daughter, niece, etc.

For a candy lover

For a Classic Valentine

For a "Sweetheart"

Figure 35

Figure 35 shows four different ideas for Valentine Bundles. The "For a young girl: daughter, niece, etc." example shows a bundle with a Hello Kitty plush toy, matching candy, toy and pink bucket. The "Candy Lover" bundle includes an M&M candy plush, a bag of M&Ms

and a treat box. For the "Classic Valentine" bundle, the example shows a red plush bear holding a rose, heart-shaped chocolates, and a basket. "For a Sweetheart" is a themed bundle that includes a sweetheart bear, candies and container. These are just ideas to get your creative juices flowing. You do not need to make bundles; individual items will also sell, just be sure to offer value to your potential Amazon buyer.

Mardi Gras party supplies including masks, beads and paper products in purple, gold and green are a big seller right now. The Mardi Gras festival season varies from city to city, but it is generally celebrated during the final three-day period before Ash Wednesday. This date fluctuates because Ash Wednesday is always 46 days before Easter, and Mardi Gras, which is French for Fat Tuesday, is always the day before Ash Wednesday.

Sales for Super Bowl parties are also strong in January because the Super Bowl is held during the first week of February. Regional items for the competing teams' home towns will sell as well as everything needed for a Super Bowl party. Think of football-themed party supplies and decor, serving pieces like bowls, platters and flatware. Assorted colors from the two competing teams are also strong sellers at this time.

For example, the 2014 Super Bowl featured the Denver Broncos and the Seattle Seahawks. Denver fans decorated with orange and blue while Seahawk's fans cheered their team to victory with navy blue and light green accessories. See Figure 36 for some great decorating ideas including solid color streamers and balloons, team logo plates and napkins with coordinating tableware.

Figure 36

Take advantage of national advertising for bedding and white sales in January (Figure 37). The major department stores will be promoting *their* merchandise and you can jump on this opportunity as well. Since people have the white sale advertising on their mind, this is a good time to sell the smaller bedding and linen sets available at your dollar store. Dollar stores have a huge assortment of bath and bedroom accessories including packs of washcloths, shower curtains and pillow cases. A few stores even carry small throw pillows.

As people freshen up their bathrooms and bedrooms during this time, it will be worthwhile for you to see what other items from your dollar store fit in with current marketing and advertising. There isn't a specific target date for this merchandise, such as February 14th for Valentine sales. People see the ads and make their plans for shopping. Buy these types of products and send them in as early as possible in January. If you are creating a listing for these items be sure to add the keywords *white sale* in addition to your other keywords.

JANUARY
WHITE
20%
OFF
SALE

Hurry in! Sale ends January 31

Figure 37

FEBRUARY is a good time to take stock of your inventory on Amazon because this is the time of year that long term storage fees are assessed. After you have taken care of that, think spring! There is a small window of opportunity for St. Patrick's Day merchandise (Figure 38) and then you are ready to gear up for Easter Sales.

Figure 38

This is a great time to "kill two birds with one stone." Parents don't really want the Easter bunny to fill their children's Easter baskets with lots of useless plastic toys. Nowadays Easter baskets are trending toward arts and crafts and other useful items like chalk, crayons and paint. Now is the time to send in supplies for back-to-school as well as for those budding young artists. Crayons, colored pencils, crafts and office supplies in fun colors can all be sold now in preparation for Easter Basket stuffing. Any leftovers will be ready for your back-to-school sales in a few months. Remember the Valentine Bundles/baskets that you created in January? Generic ones (that aren't specifically "I love you") will also work well as Easter Basket gifts. Take a look at the Hello Kitty bundle from Figure 35. Leave it as is or add a few filled eggs and jelly beans to magically transform it into an adorable Easter gift (figure 39). If you decide to make this change, you will need to request that Amazon return your current Hello Kitty bundles so that you can make changes and create a new listing with the appropriate keywords and updated information.

Figure 39

MARCH promises to come in like a lion and go out like a lamb, so this is a good time to send in any Spring-themed merchandise. As people start thinking about spring cleaning and freshening up their home after a long winter, storage bins, organizers of all shapes and sizes, and other household items for storing winter articles are strong sellers in early spring.

APRIL showers bring May flowers and May brings Mother's Day so get ready for lots of love for Mom by sending in *any* gift items. Whenever you send in items that are appropriate for gift giving, be sure to add keywords that will target the recipient: "gifts for her," "gifts for mom," "Mother's Day," etc. Keep current with Mother's Day advertising. For example, if your favorite store circular is advertising lots of daisy patterned décor, look at your dollar store for things that fit with that trend like the towel shown in Figure 40.

Figure 40

MAY is a great time to gear up for Father's Day and Graduation time.

June will bring "Dads and Grads" advertising (Figure 41) and also the end of the school year and the beginning of summer. So get ready to take advantage of all of the advertising to come.

Figure 41

Beach toys will be a "hot" item soon. Your best bet is summer inflatables because these will be small items, easy to ship to Amazon. You can also send in plastic beach buckets filled with sand toys and other summer-specific items, just keep in mind that larger items will cost you more money to ship and store at Amazon. **Waterproof** is a great keyword at this time of year. Check your dollar store for cases and containers that will keep electronics dry as people hit the beach and pool this summer.

JUNE is the time to celebrate America with as much red, white and blue as you can shake a flag at. You want to be ready with merchandise that can be used for 4th of July celebrations as well Labor Day in September. Patriotic party supplies will never go out of style and are used year-round for military celebrations, Memorial Day, July 4th, Labor Day and Veteran's Day observances.

In presidential election years, you will also see a spike in "red, white and blue" sales leading up to November's Election Day. If you ever find merchandise with the Democratic Donkey or Republican Elephant, buy everything you can. I sold dozens of Republican Elephant paper products (Figure 42) during the last major election.

Figure 42

JULY is a great time to send in birthday supplies. Many summer birthdays are celebrated outside since there is less of a threat of rain than in the spring and fall. Paper products, favors, invitations and thank you cards can be found in many dollar stores. Once again these present wonderful bundling opportunities. Also, plenty of families travel during the summer while the kids are home from school, so travel items sell very well now. Look for travel games for kids and any items for the air traveler (luggage tags, locks, travel cosmetic kits, etc).

A different set of shoppers is hitting Amazon looking for dorm supplies. College classes generally begin session before public schools so there are some specific items that these back-to-school/college-bound shoppers need. Many retail stores that have nearby colleges publish lists of must-have dorm items. Grab one of these sheets and look for products that you can purchase from the dollar store and add the keywords **dorm, college**, etc. to these listings. A great resource is the *Bed, Bath and Beyond* website. They have a *College* tab that lists many colleges around the nation and their preferred list of items recommended by their individual Campus Residence Associations. Search the lists and find products at dollar stores (Figure 43).

WHAT TO BRING

Organize	
Under-the-bed storage container	✓
Storage crates/ utility bins	✓
Sweater and/or shoe organizer	✓
Bulletin board/ dry erase board	✓
Memo board (for student's door)	✓
Over-the door-mirror	✓
Wall safe adhesive (3M) - for hanging posters, pictures	✓
Cleaning supplies, broom, dust pan	✓
Hand vacuum	✓
First aid kit, Small sewing kit, Tool kit, Flashlight/ batteries	✓
Umbrella	✓
Shower	
Towels & washcloths (suggest 2 to 3 sets)	✓
Bathrobe, Shower shoes/ flip flops	✓
Shower caddy	✓
Toiletries	✓
Make-up or shaving mirror	✓
Hair dryer	✓
Electric curling iron (with auto shut-off)	✓
Electric razor	✓
Electric toothbrush	✓
If room has an attached bathroom - Soap dish, shower curtain/rings, bath rug	✓

Figure 43

Electronic accessories will be big sellers as well as some standard items that the typical college student will need

118

while living away from home: kitchen items, bathroom supplies, bedding and personal items. Leaving home means doubling up on items that were previously taken for granted. That off-campus apartment probably needs everything from tissue boxes to shower curtains and hooks.

AUGUST is back-to-school sales time for the brick-and-mortar stores but you sent in these types of items when you sent in supplies for Easter baskets so you are all set. Now is when you should really starting gearing up for your 4th quarter holiday sales. Don't wait! Lots of people who work in the retail and customer service industries will be shopping online. They'll soon be working so many hours in the mall, standing on their feet and dealing with customers that it is unlikely they'll go shopping after work. When I worked in retail, I made sure that the bulk of my personal Christmas shopping was done before the end of October. However, with the explosive growth of online shopping, many people find it easier to shop online and be done. Have your products positioned at Amazon's warehouse early so that you can sell to these shoppers.

As an online seller, you want your holiday merchandise ready for sale and at the fulfillment centers as early as possible. Think about the number of other FBA sellers who will also be sending in merchandise to Amazon's warehouses as the holiday season approaches. Amazon employees will do their best and additional seasonal staff is hired to work in the Amazon warehouses to process shipments but why should you have your products tied up in all of that? Get your items in early and add to your supply as you sell out. At the very least, you want all of your items on Amazon's warehouse shelves for Black Friday which means they need to be sent in to Amazon by the first week of November.

SEPTEMBER sees the kids off to school and the parents taking a collective sigh of relief. Some dollar stores will begin to have summer clearance sales. Whether or not yours does, stock up on summer toys, especially inflatables, kids' goggles and other smaller pool gear. Stick to items that sold well for you throughout the summer. Often, families plan vacations for the fall or winter and will require pool gear that is not available anywhere but online. Have you ever tried to buy a bathing suit in January? It's not easy.

September in the dollar store also means fun Halloween accessories. This is another great time to look at what the circulars are advertising. If princesses are wearing pink and yellow, look for accessories to match. You don't need to have a Disney kid in your house to see the trends in the stores. Children will want costumes based on recent movie releases and any accessories related to those movies will sell well now.

Pirate accessories are always a safe bet. Keep an eye on the quality of these accessories, go for the better looking items. Don't waste your money on items you wouldn't give to your own children (Figure 44).

Figure 44

When you are making your decision about costume accessory possibilities, go back to one of your original keys to success in the dollar store: What items look too good to be in a dollar store? The cheap toys will still be cheap toys but the pirate eye patch, telescope and earring could be promising. Think about themed bundles. These accessories sell for lots of money at those seasonal Halloween stores that pop up for two months each year. Visit one before visiting your dollar store and you will be amazed at the difference in what accessories cost.

OCTOBER begins with Fire Prevention Week in some areas and ends with candy on October 31st. What's not to love? Continue to send in holiday items based on "Low Inventory Alerts" from Amazon in Seller Central. This is also a great time to send in Calendars from the dollar store. The small "checkbook" size pocket calendars and wall calendars still sell even though most people have calendars on their phones. Be careful you don't over-buy calendars. They do not sell well after January and calendars are readily available at many other stores. There is a great opportunity to find ones at the dollar store that are a little different from those available from other retailers. Last year my local dollar store had a selection of baby animal calendars, classic cars calendars and a calendar of beaches from around the world. They all sold by mid-December. The beach-themed calendar in Figure 45 actually came with a smaller desk-sized calendar. They sold well, but again, don't over-buy.

Figure 45

October also brings thoughts of a picture–perfect Thanksgiving dinner. Reality may set in sometime in November, but while the dream is alive, send in serving pieces that will complement a fall holiday table. The entire family converges on one household so that means additional flatware, napkins, dishes and serving pieces will sell.

NOVEMBER is a time for family and friends. Here in the northeast, I enjoy the "shoof–shoof" sound of walking through the fallen leaves.   Now get out of my way, I have shopping to do! Actually, there is no need to scramble to buy product to send to Amazon. Your dollar store purchases are still selling and you are keeping an eye on your "Low Inventory Alerts."

Look carefully at your best-selling items right now and raise prices to stay competitive. That's right, I said RAISE prices. Demand is very high at this time of year and your stock will run out quickly if they are priced too low. Replenish (send to Amazon) any products that you can. Look at the Christmas ornaments that are now being displayed at your dollar store. You still have time to send these in for people to use for their holiday decorating.

DECEMBER is the time to clear out any older merchandise. Adjust prices to get rid of any slow moving inventory. If something has been listed since January with little interest, lower the price and move on. This is your best shot to get rid of extra merchandise before February fees are assessed. Let your wall calendar inventory run out. You only paid a dollar each but why throw away dollars on stock that won't sell after the New Year? Speaking of the New Year, New Year's party supplies will sell soon so send them in to Amazon as early as you can in December.

Buy anything related to exercise and anything resolution-oriented is a good idea this month. January first brings out the optimist in everyone as they resolve to eat less, save money, exercise more and enjoy life. The dollar store has the liquidated inventory of last year's optimism so take advantage of that merchandise. Send these items in right up to January first because people will now be buying for themselves rather than as gifts for others.

Remember that Amazon gift cards will be burning a hole in shoppers' pockets by December 26. Gift cards fit nicely in greeting cards and Christmas stockings so they are popular gifts. Amazon makes it even easier with e-gift cards that can be sent electronically. With the click of a mouse an Amazon gift card up to $2000 can be sent e-mail delivery in a variety of styles and designs.

In 2014 the average shopper spent more than $170 on gift card purchases and 62% of consumers asked for a gift card for the holidays in 2014. The Amazon Gift card was #2 of the top 10 most-searched-for gift cards. The

VISA gift card was #1 and it can also be used on Amazon! Because of this, Amazon sales tend to stay strong through the first week or two of January.

Key points from this chapter:

1. Consider the lead time needed for items to arrive at Amazon and be available for sale from the FBA warehouses.
2. Shop for similar items to those advertised at major retailers.
3. Consider individual items as well as bundles.
4. Be aware of the retail calendar and how fourth quarter sales are strong through January.

Money: Profit, Margin and ROI

This is your money, so it is important to see where your profits are and what items bring you the most return on your investment. There are programs that figure out which items of your inventory are most profitable but it is important that you know how to calculate it yourself.

$$\text{Gross Profit = Revenue - Cost of Goods Sold}$$

$$\text{Gross Profit Margin} = \frac{\text{Gross Profit}}{\text{Revenue}}$$

Figure 46

Figure 46 shows the difference between your **Gross Profit** and your **Gross Profit Margin**. Your Gross Profit Margin will be represented as a percentage. Your Cost of Goods Sold includes your Amazon fees so your Cost of Goods Sold as an Amazon seller can be calculated as your Revenue minus your cost + Amazon Fees. This becomes clearer when you fill in your numbers.

As an example, if your Mickey Mouse toy sells for **$10** (your **Revenue**) and your **Cost of Goods Sold** (your dollar store cost of $1 plus the $4.19 in Amazon fees) is $5.19, you can see in Figure 47 that your **Gross Profit is** $4.81. Now you take that **Gross Profit** amount and divide it by your **Revenue** (which is your payout from Amazon) to find your **Gross Profit Margin**. $4.81 / $10 = 0.481 which is approximately **48%**. (Figure 47).

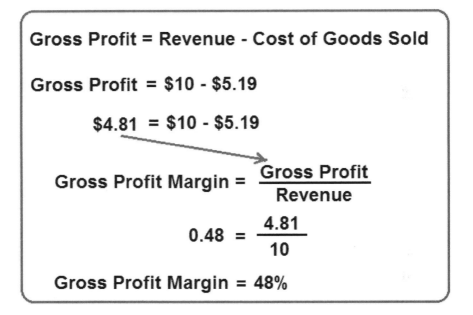

Gross Profit = Revenue - Cost of Goods Sold

Gross Profit = $10 - $5.19

$4.81 = $10 - $5.19

Gross Profit Margin = $\frac{\text{Gross Profit}}{\text{Revenue}}$

$0.48 = \frac{4.81}{10}$

Gross Profit Margin = 48%

Figure 47

So you paid a dollar and at the end of the day you have made a profit of $4.81. Your profit margin is 48%, not bad at all. Gross Profit Margin is important because two people can have the same profit on an item but that doesn't tell you who made the better investment. I know this involves math, but stay with me here.

As an example, let's suppose Jim and Deb each made a profit of $15 on the sale of one item. It looks like they have both done well, however, a closer look shows that Deb made the better investment. Deb spent $5 on her purchase to make $15 so her margin will look like Figure 48.

$$\frac{\$15 - \$5}{\$15} = \frac{10}{15} = .66 = 66\% \ \textbf{Margin}$$

Figure 48

But Jim spent $12 on his purchase to make his $15. Jim's gross profit margin therefore looks like Figure 49.

$$\frac{\$15 - \$12}{\$15} = \frac{3}{15} = .20 = 20\% \ \textbf{Margin}$$

Figure 49

Clearly, 66% is greater than 20% but what does that really mean? It means that for every dollar generated in sales, Deb makes 66¢ in profit. On the other hand, for every dollar that Jim generates in sales, he makes only 20¢ in profit. This shows much more clearly that Deb made a better investment and that Jim needs to spend more money on his products to make the same $15 at the end of the day.

Another way that we look at the profits from our purchases is by looking at the ROI (Return on Investment). Mickey Mouse sells for $10 and his cost (including Amazon fees) is $5.19. In Figure 50 you can see that the **ROI** is calculated by subtracting your **cost** of **$5.19** from your **revenue** of **$10** and dividing that result by your **cost** of **$5.19**. This result is represented as a percentage. Your **ROI** for Mickey Mouse is **92.6%.**

$$ROI = \frac{Revenue - Cost}{Cost}$$

$$ROI = \frac{\$10.00 - \$5.19}{\$5.19} = \frac{4.81}{5.19}$$

$$ROI = .926 = 92.6\% \text{ return on investment}$$

Figure 50

What exactly does ROI mean? Let's say that our revenue was the same as our cost. That means we broke even, which would look like Figure 51.

$$ROI = \frac{Revenue - Cost}{Cost}$$

$$ROI = \frac{\$10.00 - \$10.00}{\$10.00} = \frac{0}{\$10.00} = 0$$

$$ROI = 0 = 0\% \text{ return on investment}$$

Figure 51

This is not an ideal scenario. You did all that work and you only broke even. In other words, you got your original money back. The previous example shows that Mickey Mouse gave you more than a 92% return on your investment. If you are trying to decide between different products to carry, look at the different ROIs and select the products that consistently give you a higher return.

What does a negative ROI mean? Since an ROI of zero means that you broke even, if the ROI is a negative number, the costs must be greater than your gains and you have **lost** money. Stay away from these items! Sometimes a loss is inevitable. Perhaps you purchased an item that stopped selling well on Amazon so you lowered your price to sell your product, but not at a profit. Perhaps another seller undercut your prices so your items didn't sell. Maybe you just made a mistake. Take the loss as a learning experience and move on to bigger and better profits.

When you have a better understanding of your margins and your ROI, you can see why I suggest that you price your items for at least $10. You want to see as much profit as possible at the end of the day. Large corporations can more easily absorb losses and thin margins. However, every dollar *you* invest needs to be carefully thought out so that you do not have money tied up in products that are not profitable or products that are bringing you small margins. This is also why I caution you to buy just a few pieces of an item if you are not sure about them. It is much easier to absorb a loss on three items rather than on 24, 48 or 100 items. So start small when selling new, untried merchandise to see how well it sells.

Take a look at all of the available information when deciding what to buy at your dollar store. You now know how to calculate your ROI, profit and margin. You can look at the sales rank of the item (if it is provided) and your current competition. Put all of this information together to buy the most profitable items you can.

Luckily, since you are focusing on making your purchases from a dollar store, each individual item has the same cost of $1, so if you find an item with a $15 sales price, you can immediately tell that it will be a better investment than an item that will only sell for $9. The higher math doesn't begin until you start creating bundles where you are putting multiple $1 items together and the cost of the bundle is $4, $5, $10 or even $20 depending upon how many items you combine.

Key points from this chapter:

1. Understand your Gross Profit and your Gross Profit Margin.
2. Know which of your items give you the best return for your money.

Tools of the Trade

I sold on eBay for more than 12 years before selling on Amazon so I already had some packing material, a computer, a smartphone and a camera. I retired my digital camera when I switched over to Amazon full time. Unless I am creating my own listing, I no longer need to photograph every item I sell. Over the years, I have upgraded my smartphone so that my photos are even better than those of that trusty digital camera. So what items do you truly NEED to be prepared to sell on Amazon?

- Smartphone
- Computer
- Laser Printer
- Scale
- Boxes & Packing Tape
- Labels (Avery 30/page)
- And of course, items to sell!

This is the bare minimum. I recommend a smartphone for research in the store. If you are really looking for a bare bones approach to use your old flip phone to call someone at home with access to a computer and have them research items for you. I say this because for some people, a new smartphone is simply not in the budget. You can make it work.

At the other end of the spectrum is the Ultimate Amazon Seller's Tools of the Trade. You can almost hear the angels singing and see the divine light shining upon your workstation. Back on earth, you have:

- Smartphone, iPhone or iPad
- Scanning program
- Scanfob or other little bluetooth scanner to use in stores (Figure 52)

Figure 52

- Laptop
- Laser printer
- Scotty peelers (Figure 53) to remove labels and price tags
- Boxes
- Tape
- Tape Measure

- Box cutter
- Poly bags with suffocation warning labels to use for plush, textiles and multi-packs
- Dymo or Zebra label printer
- Rolls of labels
- Desktop scanner

Figure 53

Your **Tools of the Trade** will vary from mine. You want to use tools that will make your job easier without breaking the bank. Last year I had four part-time employees during the spring and summer. This year I only had one and also outsourced all of my accounting. I don't think those employees would be happy being called "tools" but I certainly needed them to make my job easier during those months.

Look at your business. What do you really want to accomplish? You have so many resources available to you but you do not need them all. I subscribe to Facebook groups that help me grow my business and I subscribe to other services that save me time and money. There are books and classes and tutorials for online selling. This is your business, find what works for you. To be successful you need to find your niche, your focus. As you move along your path to success, buy tools that make it easier to run your business.

Since you are running a business, be sure to get an EIN (Employer Identification Number) also known as a Federal Tax Identification Number which is used to identify a business entity. In general, businesses need an EIN. You may apply for an EIN in various ways, and now you may apply online. This is a free service offered by the Internal Revenue Service and you can get your EIN immediately.

You must check with your individual state to see if you need a state number or charter. Here in New Jersey I was required to register my business with the state. One huge benefit to completing this process early, is that you generally need your EIN to use a resale certificate which allows you to purchase, tax free, items that you plan to resell. Oh yeah, you also avoid getting into trouble with the IRS.

So, get a tax ID (EIN) and ask each store how they handle tax exempt purchases. Some require a copy of your tax ID certificate. Learn your state's rules and each store's rules. Fill out the state-provided paperwork for your state. Google "resale certificate" and your state, to see how simple the form really is. I actually keep a few blank copies of New Jersey's ST-3 Resale Certificate in my car in case I need them. Some store employees don't do this very often so occasionally it can take a long time. If the tax savings are not worth the time, pay and move on. You can request credit for sales tax later but don't pay it upfront if you don't need to. If this seems confusing, find a local CPA to help.

Key points from this chapter:

1. Start with the items you absolutely need to run your business.
2. Add tools and services to help you succeed.
3. If you haven't done so already, get an EIN and use a Resale Certificate when you shop to avoid paying sales tax on items you plan to resell.

Know When to Hold 'em and When to Fold 'em

Kenny Rogers is known as "The Gambler" but you don't have to be. You have learned how to use the available information to make good purchasing decisions. As with much of life, however, you may still find that things just didn't work out the way you planned. Now what? There are certainly many options available to you. Can you lower the price of your items? Adjust your keywords? Make some other changes to get your inventory to sell? Perhaps your items simply will not sell. You have the option of removing these items and having them sent back to you, or you ask Amazon to dispose of them to avoid being charged storage fees on unprofitable merchandise. Figure 53 shows the Amazon fees as of summer 2015.

Inventory Removal Orders		
Service	Per Standard-Size* Unit	Per Oversize* Unit
Return	$0.50	$0.60
Disposal	$0.15	$0.30

All prices include the cost of shipping.

Important: Removal orders may not be used to fulfill customer orders.

* Standard-Size includes anv packaaed Unit that is 20 lb. or less with its longest side 18 inches or less, its shortest side 8 inches or less, and its median side 14 inches or less.

A Unit exceeding any of these dimensions is Oversize.

Figure 53

For every item you want to have returned to you, Amazon charges 50¢ per item and only 15¢ for disposal of items. There is no additional shipping charged on items returned to you. Oversized units are charged 60¢ for return and 30¢ for disposal. Compare this to the long term storage fees you may be assessed and make the decisions for your own merchandise.

I prefer to have my products returned to me so that I can donate them to a local charity. The decision is entirely up to you. In general, you want to avoid paying long term storage fees in February and August, and also avoid losing money on your purchases. Personally, I hold on to seasonal items that I know will sell well in a few months, but other than that, I avoid paying for long term storage. Sometimes losing money is inevitable, so learn from any mistakes and move on. Even buyers for the best retail stores make mistakes.

You can subscribe to programs that make managing and repricing your inventory much easier. These programs continue to improve and change, so do your own research to see which of these programs work best for you.

Finally, "Sponsored Products" is an advertising service that helps you promote the products you list on Amazon.com. Amazon wants you to sell products and has a variety of options for you to choose from.

Key points from this chapter:

1. Sometimes items don't sell.
2. Changing your listing may help sell your item.
3. Know when it is time to have the item removed from Amazon.
4. Learn from your mistakes and move on.

Movie Tie-Ins

I love selling products that tie in with popular movies. Before we talk specifically about dollar store items, let's take a look at movie tie-in merchandise as a whole. Movie tie-in merchandise is any merchandise sold to help promote a movie. This is an especially lucrative market for movies geared toward children. What would a Disney movie be without princess dolls showing up on every shelf at Target, Walmart and every store in between? Movie merchandise includes clothing, toys, posters, figurines, action figures, collectible replicas and even Christmas ornaments.

Wait, what? Why would a summer blockbuster movie have Christmas ornaments? If you visit your local Hallmark store when they display their Christmas ornaments, you will see plenty of Star Trek and Star Wars themed ornaments. The simple reason you will find them is because they sell. People have favorite movies and TV shows and they are happy to buy little reminders of them.

A perfect example of this is the animated movie "Toy Story" (Figure 54). Toy Story 3 was released in 2010 yet Toy Story characters, party supplies and clothing still sell well. The characters are timeless and lovable and new children are introduced to the franchise all the time. A new installment of the franchise is scheduled for release in June of 2017. Expect a huge surge in all things Toy Story when that new movie hits theaters.

Figure 54

So when is the best time to sell your movie themed inventory?

There are generally three peak times for the sales of movie tie-in merchandise. Regardless of the time of year, whether a movie is released as a summer blockbuster or on a random weekend in the fall, movie-related merchandise—especially for movies geared toward children—will have at least three peak sales times:

1. When the movie is released in theater.
2. When the movie is released on Blu-ray and DVD
3. At least one Christmas season

In addition, children's movie-themed party supplies sell well in spring and summer when home birthday parties are on the rise.

Let's take the example of Walt Disney Pictures "Wreck-It Ralph" (Figure 55). This animated movie went into general release at theaters on November 2, 2012. It earned $471 million in worldwide box office revenue, $189 million of that in the United States and Canada. Retailers immediately released toys and paper party supplies to tie in with the movie—after all, it was Disney. However, with Christmas shelf space at a premium, "Wreck-It Ralph" product was quickly discounted and sold. Party supplies were on clearance before the movie was even out of the theaters.

Figure 55

"Wreck-It Ralph" was released on Blu-ray and DVD on March 5, 2013. By that time, small amounts of merchandise were available and paper products were practically non-existent. Some children were seeing "Wreck-It Ralph" for the first time but could not easily get toy tie-ins from local retailers. "Oz the Great and Powerful" was released on March 8, 2013 and stores packed their shelves with merchandise from this much-anticipated new release from Disney. The animated "Wreck-It Ralph" characters of Ralph, Felix and

Vanellope (Figure 55) were overshadowed by the 3D fantasy adventure film "Oz". But stop for a moment. Young children were unlikely to see the PG-rated "Oz the Great and Powerful" and were begging their parents for candy cars (Figure 56) and "We can fix it" themed toys.

Figure 56

FBA to the rescue! Oh, the wonderful world of online sales. Online merchants had a huge advantage here. Any sellers who still had merchandise could command a price well above retail for these toys since they simply were not available anywhere else.

"Wreck-It Ralph" was just being seen by millions of children but the brick-and-mortar retailers had moved on and even party supplies were non-existent. The following summer, just three months after the DVD release, toys that had originally sold for $24.99 climbed to more than $100! Fewer than 100 units of any specific toy were available and nearly all were selling at prices higher than their original suggested retail price. By this time, party supplies were practically non-existent.

The website Camel Camel Camel is an Amazon price tracker that provides price drop alerts and price history charts for products sold by Amazon. The price history charts on www.camelcamelcamel.com for "Wreck-It Ralph" toys showed sales peaks at the following times:

- Original theatrical release
- Christmas
- Blu-ray/DVD release
- Easter
- Summer birthday parties

Figure 57 shows the biggest spike in this particular Vanellope doll occurred the week of March 18, 2013 about two weeks after "Wreck-It Ralph" was released on Blu-ray and DVD.

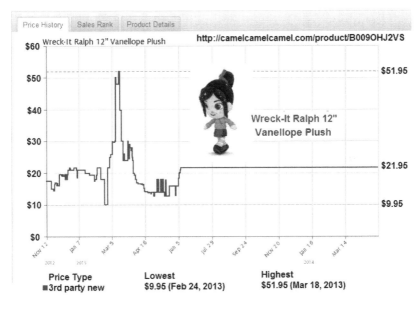

Figure 57

Movie tie ins are certainly not limited to toys and they aren't even limited to officially licensed merchandise. When "Pirates of the Caribbean" was released, ALL pirate merchandise saw a surge in sales: toys, collectibles, party supplies and costumes for children, adults and even dogs! This is very good news for the dollar store shopper. If a new princess movie is getting lots of attention, even dollar store princess items will sell. Certainly a generic wand isn't going to sell for the same amount of money as an officially licensed Disney "Frozen" wand, but there is still room for sales in general.

Never underestimate the power of a sequel. As I mentioned before, Toy Story 4 is scheduled for release in 2017. You can currently find some Toy Story merchandise from the original three movies on your dollar store shelves. You may not want to purchase them now to hold for two years but keep an eye on them. When advertising begins, buy as much as you can, the movie is sure to be a hit.

Key points from this chapter:

1. Know about the peak times for movie tie-in sales.
2. Be aware of the current movies, especially children's movies.
3. Sales are not limited to officially licensed merchandise.
4. Never underestimate the power of a sequel.

Taking It to the Next Level

You can see that making $100 per day from dollar store purchases and sales is not only possible but easy once you begin. Making $200, $300 and up to $1000 per day is not that much harder to do. You can **scale** your business by finding successful items and then repeating the process. **Scaling** means that you have a growth in revenue without a significant increase in your operating costs or in the work involved. Moving from $100 per day to $200 per day may even be easier than getting up to that original $100. It may be easier because you know which of your dollar store items are successful on Amazon and now you can find similar products to offer.

Let's look at my payout from a day in July (Figure 58). Typically, July is a slower sales month for me. On this particular day, I missed the $100 mark by pennies with a profit that day of $99.78. I am not the least bit worried since my dollar store sales skyrocket around Easter, again in the fall, and leading up to the holidays.

Product Details	Cost	Amazon Listing Price	Total Promotional Rebates	Amazon Fees	Other	Payout from Amazon
Set of 2 Girl Religious Ducks	.50	$9.99	$0.00	-$4.17	$0.00	$5.82
2 Piece Rooster Placemats	2.00	$12.00	$0.00	-$5.98	$1.51	$7.53
Baby Shower Party Bundle	11.00	$35.00	$0.00	-$9.27	$0.00	$25.73
Clothespin Hanger	1.00	$9.99	$0.00	-$4.04	$0.00	$5.95
8 Count Princess Invitations	6.00	$24.12	$0.00	-$16.24	$0.00	$7.88
8 Count Princess Invitations	2.00	$8.04	$0.00	-$6.08	$0.00	$1.96
2 Piece Kitchen Towels	2.00	$12.00	$0.00	-$6.80	$2.33	$7.53
Ceramic Duck Jewelry Holder	1.00	$15.00	-$2.53	-$4.92	$2.53	$10.08
Tied Dyed Head Bands	1.00	$10.00	$0.00	-$9.65	$5.48	$5.83
2 Piece Rooster Placemats	2.00	$12.00	$0.00	-$4.47	$0.00	$7.53
2 Piece Butterfly Placemats	2.00	$12.00	$0.00	-$4.47	$0.00	$7.53
Tie Dyed Head Bands	2.00	$20.00	$0.00	-$7.34	$0.00	$12.66
Set of 2 Girl Religious Ducks	.50	$9.99	$0.00	-$4.17	$0.00	$5.82
Set of 2 Girl Religious Ducks	.50	$9.99	$0.00	-$4.17	$0.00	$5.82
Tie Dyed Head Bands	2.00	$20.00	$0.00	-$7.34	$0.00	$12.66
Garfield Party Plates	1.00	$9.99	$0.00	-$4.04	$0.00	$5.95

My total COST from the Dollar Store ⟹ $36.50   Total payout from Amazon ⟹ $136.28

Figure 58

This example shows ten unique dollar store products that brought in more than $100 in sales on that day. It's a great place to start. Imagine this screenshot is **your** payout. What if you had 20 additional items with similar sales? You would see a return of $200 on that day. Now look more closely at the products that sold to see what you may be able to duplicate.

First, you see that a pair of religious mini ducks sold well. These were a lone winner. Further research of other rubber ducks shows that none can turn such a reliable profit and certainly none from a dollar store.

The next item on the list is a set of rooster placemats. A quick look at the Amazon listing shows a rooster atop a vintage barn. Does your dollar store have additional rooster–themed placemats? Go look, I'll wait. Better yet, start a Shopping List of things to look for at your local dollar stores. You may want to add the more general term **rooster kitchen items** to your List to see what else you may find while shopping.

The next item from Figure 58 is a bundle of baby shower party supplies. On Amazon, do a search for "party supplies bundle." Browse through the listings until you see a pattern that you recognize from your local dollar store. Maybe you will see a baby shower pattern or a football team pattern that catches your eye. Check the listing to see **exactly** what is included in the Amazon listing. Remember to check the Sales Rank of the bundle to see if it is worth trying to sell. If it looks promising, add those items to your Shopping List as well. The next step is to do a search of that exact title to see if there are other party supplies that may be selling individually or as bundles on Amazon. Why create a new listing if you don't have to?

For example, if you found a listing in your "party supplies bundle" search that had the title "Mini Gold Football Party Supplies Bundle," then search "Mini Gold Football Party" on Amazon. You may find a different bundle or even a football centerpiece that matches the items from the bundle and sells for $10 or more. Add this to your growing Shopping List.

You may notice in Figure 58 that an 8-count of Princess Invitations sold. I would not buy these again. They sold in multiples, meaning that someone bought six 8-count packs of invitations and then someone else bought two 8-count packs. The problem is that the payout was only $1.88 on the sale of six and was actually a loss on the sale of two. There was a profit of $1.84, but $1.84 on the sale of eight individual items is not worth your time. It would be much better to sell one ceramic duck jewelry holder for a profit of $9.08.

Keep adding to your Shopping List as you look at your successful product sales. Now take that Shopping List to your local dollar stores. I find it helpful to make notes that remind me which dollar store carries which products. Purchase a few of each of the products you find and list these on Amazon. Those products that sell well for you are the ones that you should replenish immediately. As you shop for replenishment items also look at new items or categories that you haven't considered before. As you become accustomed to the layout of your favorite dollar stores and the items they offer, you will notice changes in the merchandise and you will see that new items "jump out at you."

Before you know it, you will have doubled your sales, then tripled them. Now is the time to really take it to the next level. Look at the tags and labels of the merchandise that you regularly sell from the dollar store. Yes, turn over the tag and look at the company that manufactures or distributes that product. Can you buy directly from that company? If so, is it economical? Making purchases directly from these companies may sound good but how does the cost of shipping affect the purchase price? Is there a high minimum order required? Consider all of the factors involved when making your buying decision.

If you can find even one or two successful companies from which to purchase dollar store items to resell, be sure to see what other items they offer on their website. Follow the strategies that have taken you this far and continue to do what is successful. If you make any mistakes along the way, consider them a learning experience and move on. Find the strategies, products and profits that work for you and repeat the process. Remember, it all began with a dollar.

The BOLO Chapter

The following pages contain BOLOs. These are items for which you want to **Be On** the **Look Out**. These are items from my inventory that I have sold over the past three years. Some of these items are completely out of stock on Amazon, others have decreased in price and still others have increased in price. I have included the ASIN number, my sales price and my cost. If the item is a bundle or multipack, you will see a cost of $2, $5 or even $12, but all of the items listed as BOLOs were originally purchased from dollar stores.

Happy Hunting!

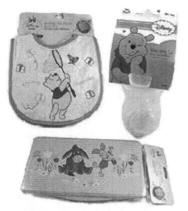

Disney Baby Winnie the Pooh
Bundle of Bib, Baby Wipes
Travel Pack, BPA-free Sippy
Cup (Pink)

ASIN: B0131KD2JQ

Sold for: $14.99
Cost: $3.00

Yogi Bear Plush Clip On

ASIN: B0052DN31S

Sold for: $9.99
Cost: $1.00

Dora the Explorer - Fantasy
Figures Princess with Dragon

ASIN: B003YMJBSS

Sold for: $12.50
Cost: $1.00

LEGO Duplo Baby Growth
Chart

ASIN: B0067RDI5E

Sold for: $9.99
Cost: $1.00

Disney Cars 2 4pk Study Kit
on Blister Card - Pencil,
Pencil Sharpener, Eraser,
Memo Pads

ASIN: B005KNVB5K

Sold for: $9.99
Cost: $1.00

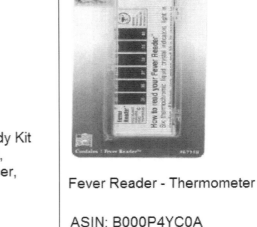

Fever Reader - Thermometer

ASIN: B000P4YC0A

Sold for: $9.99
Cost: $1.00

New York Yankees 2007 Upper
Deck Ford F-150 1/87 Scale
MLB Diecast Truck w/ Sticker

ASIN: B001TF0FPK

Sold for: $9.99
Cost: $1.00

Flex Neck Reading Light
(Purple with Pink Dots)

ASIN: 1599851520

Sold for: $10.00
Cost: $1.00

Craftsman Hauler Truck
Pez Dispenser

ASIN: B00727ECVC

Sold for $12.99
Cost: $1.00

Disney Cars Mini Stapler
with Staples on Shaped
Blister Card

ASIN: B005LA5AWC

Sold for $9.99
Cost: $1.00

Candy Cane Lane Green Holiday
Tea Decaf 20 Tea Bags

ASIN: B000I0VLUK

Sold for $12.50
Cost: $1.00

Rudolph the Red Nose
Reindeer Grow A-Sponge
Santa

ASIN: B0070Y0DQ0

Sold for $14.99
Cost: $1.00

High School Musical Party Picks 12ct

ASIN: B001DY2IWK

Sold for $9.88
Cost: $1.00

Disney / Pixar CARS Movie Accessory Tabbed Notepad

ASIN: B0015QZZBM

Sold for $9.00
Cost: $1.00

High School Musical 3 Molded Candle

ASIN: B0017IJY5G

Sold for $11.00
Cost: $1.00

Kung Fu Panda '2' Plastic Table Cover (1ct)

ASIN: B004U9XERS

Sold for $10.49
Cost: $1.00

Christmas Goose Counted Cross Stitch Kit

ASIN: B001J8QJM0

Sold for $9.89
Cost: $1.00

Janlynn Pooh Mini Counted X-Stitch Kit

ASIN: B001DEEGZM

Sold for $9.99
Cost: $1.00

Crayola Sprayer Refills (Use with the Wonder Sprayer)

ASIN: B000NU2LHW

Sold for $11.49
Cost: $1.00

Maxell : Video Std Grade VHS 160 min GX Silver - Total of 2 Each

ASIN: B002ZZ3E1A

Sold for $14.00
Cost: $2.00

Holmes H100 2-Pack Humidifier Replacement Filters with Microban (Arm & Hammer Odor Eliminator) Fits HM729, HM 630, HM4600

ASIN: B0040IEGCQ

Sold for $10.90
Cost: $1.00

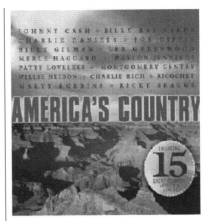

America's Country CD
Original recording remastered

ASIN: B000063DG6

Sold for $9.99
Cost: $1.00

How to Train Your Dragon Lunch Napkins (16 Count)

ASIN: B003ALFY3Y

Sold for $9.49
Cost: $1.00

The Incredible Hulk Coloring & Activity Book

ASIN: B001BUKK26

Sold for $10.00
Cost: $1.00

Tee Time Golf Banner Plastic

ASIN: B001NDMWIQ

Sold for $9.99
Cost: $1.00

Chia Pet Kung Fu Panda 2 - Po Decorative Planter

ASIN: B001JH1SZO

Sold for $25.00
Cost: $1.00

Looney Tunes Tweety Bird Valentine's Day Plastic Snowglobe Waterball

ASIN: B0072ZVAGY

Sold for $15.00
Cost: $1.00

Zhu Zhu Puppies Zhu Zhu Puppy Legend

ASIN: B004ZOTGVQ

Sold for $10.99
Cost: $1.00

Limited Edition Nips Eggnog 4 Oz (Pack of Three)

ASIN: B006YBEZSW

Sold for $25.00
Cost: $3.00

Thomas and Friends Mini Coloring Banners ~ Color Your Own Banners

ASIN: B00725X3J6

Sold for $12.00
Cost: $1.00

Fiesta Printed Party Confetti 1/2oz

ASIN: B000GKXWT0

Sold for $10.00
Cost: $1.00

Fiesta Flashing Pin

ASIN: B001K32B3A

Sold for $10.00
Cost: $1.00

Spiced Apple Cider - Instant
Drink Mix, 5 packets,(Lottie &
Beck)

ASIN: B006NI6KMU

Sold for $10
Cost: $1.00

Super Mario Brothers Nintendo
3 Dees Gummy Candy
Theater Box

ASIN: B0041NADZY

Sold for $9.00
Cost $1.00

HEDLEY'S-GREEN TEA 40ct

ASIN: B002GHWBBQ

Sold for $12.00
Cost: $1.00

Green Plaid Golf Journal

ASIN: B001CCA226

Sold for $10.49
Cost: $1.00

Star Wars Anakin Skywalker
Light up Yo-yo

ASIN: B006UNZCHC

Sold for $9.99
Cost $1.00

The Last Airbender -
Aang's Battle Staff

ASIN: B0036WT0U0

Sold for $15.00
Cost: $1.00

Sock Monkey 24 piece Sock
Monkey Birthday Lenticular
Puzzle

ASIN: B006KQ4GOY

Sold for $10.00
Cost: $1.00

Circuit Electronics Wrist Pad
For Mouse

ASIN: B002RGRXZA

Sold for $8.99
Cost: $1.00

Wilton Fairies Candle Set
2811-3330

ASIN: B0049WDBSI

Sold for $15.00
Cost: $1.00

Set of 2 Elegant Tulips & Easter
Rabbits Kitchen Dish Towels

ASIN: B00T1752JM

Sold for $17.00
Cost: $2.00

Sassy Mam Soccer Sport
Orthodontic Latex Pacifier Set
of 2

ASIN: B00349H96W

Sold for $9.99
Cost: $1.00

Disney Pixar CARS Inflatable
Boxing Gloves NIB Boxer

ASIN: B006MMBU0Y

Sold for $12.00
Cost: $1.00

Nukote Black and Red
Calculator Ink Rollers For
EL2192 - Rollers

ASIN: B003R0SGPG

Sold for $13.00
Cost: $1.00

Dog Discover Pack, Golden
Retriever

ASIN: B002KW3M1A

Sold for $10.99
Cost: $1.00

Pocket Parafoil Kites

ASIN: B0070P8L6S

Sold for $8.99
Cost: $1.00

Deck of 78 Tarot Cards -
Instructional Booklet Included

ASIN: B007AHMBQW

Sold for $12.00
Cost: $1.00

Thomas the Tank Birthday
Party Supplies - Treat Box

ASIN: B0054DA23I

Sold for $11.50
Cost: $1.00

Cupcake Party Pack:
Graduation

ASIN: B003T33HPU

Sold for $12.50
Cost: $1.00

Great Expectations Beverage
Napkins 36ct

ASIN: B0028MZCEW

Sold for $12.00
Cost: $1.00

Golden 50th Anniversary
Dessert Plates 8ct

ASIN: B001QI4EIO

Sold for $15.00
Cost: $1.00

Thanksgiving Turkey Gobble Gobble 4 Piece Kitchen
Set - Oven Mitt, Pot Holder, 2 Decorative Towels

ASIN: B00F3BIDO6

Sold for $25.00
Cost: $3.00

Disney Frozen Party Supplies for 8; Invitations, Thank You
Cards, Confetti, Tableware and Decorations

ASIN: B00L9F9RU4

Sold for $45.00
Cost: $12.00

Glossary and Abbreviations

4th quarter – Refers to October, November and December which is traditionally the strongest time of year for retail sales.

Amazon A-to-Z Guarantee – This simply states that the condition of the item a customer buys and its timely delivery are guaranteed by Amazon.

Amazon Prime – A paid service that gives Amazon shoppers Prime Member benefits including free two-day shipping on any eligible item without a minimum-order requirement, video streaming through Amazon Prime Instant Video, and other member-only perks.

Amazon Seller App – A free app from Amazon that lets you scan product barcodes to see current prices on Amazon.

App – Application; typically a small, specialized program downloaded onto mobile devices.

Arbitrage – The practice of taking advantage of a price difference between two or more markets.

Black Friday – The day after Thanksgiving.

Bluetooth Scanner – A small scanner that links wirelessly to your smartphone and quickly scans barcodes.

Bundle – A group of similar products sold together in one listing.

Buy deep – Purchase in larger quantities.

Camel Camel Camel – An Amazon price tracker site that provides price drop alerts and price history charts for products sold by Amazon. www.camelcamelcamel.com

Cost of Goods Sold – The actual amount you paid for an item that you purchased for resale).

Dollar Store – A specialty store where each item sells for $1.00.

EIN or FEIN – A Federal Tax Identification Number used to identify a business entity.

FBA – Fulfillment by Amazon. You store your products in Amazon's fulfillment centers, and they pick, pack, ship and provide customer service for these products.

Gross Profit – Your revenue minus your cost of goods sold.

Gross Profit Margin – Your gross profit divided by your revenue and represented as a percent.

HAZMAT – Hazardous material; a material or substance that poses a danger to life, property, or the environment.

ISBN – An abbreviation for International Standard Book Number (similar to a UPC) that uniquely identifies books.

Mini bundles – Bundles of just two or three items.

Online Arbitrage – Buying products online to resell for a profit.

Poly bag – A polyethylene bag; basically a plastic bag used to store or protect food or other items.

QR codes – Quick Response Codes. These look like a grid and store lots of data.

Replenish – To restock merchandise by sending it into Amazon's fulfillment center.

Revenue – Income from the sale of products.

RGB – Red, Green, Blue; refers to a system for representing the colors used on a computer display.

ROI – Return on Investment; calculated as revenue minus cost divided by cost and represented as a percent.

Sales Rank – An Amazon figure that indicates how recently an item has sold.

Scaling – Having a growth in revenue without a significant increase in operating costs or in the work involved.

ScanPower – A subscription service with many valuable features that sellers can use "to maximize their efficiency and increase their margins (and profits) by utilizing the best data." www.scanpower.com

Seller Central – The Amazon webpage where you view and manage your inventory and orders.

Suffocation Warning – "WARNING: To avoid danger of suffocation, keep this plastic bag away from babies and children. Do not use this bag in cribs, beds, carriages or play pens. This bag is not a toy."

Third-party seller – A seller who is not employed by a company (such as eBay or Amazon) and who is the owner of the merchandise.

UPC – Universal Product Code; a barcode that is widely used for tracking products in stores.

Made in the USA
Middletown, DE
12 November 2015